Design of Rehabilitation Services
In Psychiatric Hospital Settings

Design of Rehabilitation Services In Psychiatric Hospital Settings

Gail S. Fidler, OTR, FAOTA

RAMSCO Publishing Company

RAMSCO Publishing Company is a subsidiary of RAM Associates LTD., P.O. Box N, Laurel, Maryland 20707.

ISBN 0-943596-05-X

Library of Congress Catalogue No. 84-60474

First Printing, April 1984

TO

Alp Karahasan, MD, PhD, whose wisdom and courageous determination made so much possible.

AND TO

Ruth Brunyate Wiemer, OTR, PhD, who with vision and skillful leadership created the climate for possibilities.

TABLE OF CONTENTS

INTRODUCTION

In September 1978, I began work as a consultant with the Mental Hygiene Administration of the Maryland State Department of Health and Mental Hygiene. Prior to this time, at the request of Ruth Wiemer, OTR, who was Chief of the Division of Occupational Therapy in the Department of Health and Mental Hygiene, I had completed a statewide survey of occupational therapy and activity therapy services and programs in the Mental Hygiene Administration. This survey confirmed that serious inadequacies and deficiencies existed in almost all aspects of patient program services. The report outlined recommendations for extensive changes in program design, organizational structure, staffing and staff use, and supervisory and administrative procedures. The report of findings and recommendations for changes in the system and in program services had been submitted to the department and discussed with Dr. Alp Karahasan, Deputy Director of the Mental Hygiene Administration (now Director), as well as with the administrative and programmatic staff at each of the institutions.

Dr. Karahasan's response to the report was to ask me to "turn the system around" and to work to develop a quality model of program services for the state hospitals. Thus, our plan was to concentrate on building model services at the Springfield Hospital Center with the long-range goal of using the hospital as a training center and model from which adaptations could be made to improve other institutions. Throughout this period, Dr. Karahasan's administrative support and professional acumen were the forces that made the system responsive to the processes of change.

Returning to the state hospital system after so many years was a sobering experience. It was like entering a time warp, as though time had stood still and nothing had changed. With few exceptions, the wards, the patients, the routines, and the staff seemed to be the same as I had left them some 30 years ago.

Where to begin? How to begin to address a number of very critical questions? How can services be organized within a hospital so that the frequently fragmented or haphazard "program happenings" are reduced? Is it possible to design and implement a system that is responsive to the schizophrenic patient's need for structure and predictability but avoids the deadly sameness of each day? Is there a more cost-effective and program-effective way of deploying existing staff? How should staffing needs be determined? How does one determine the priorities of service when needs are so numerous? *How does one begin to mainstream rehabilitation into a hospital?* In the plethora of therapies, can unique expertise be described for each discipline? These were only some of the many questions that had to be addressed in the process of establishing services and bringing about change.

The materials in this book then were developed in response to some of these questions; in response to the need to have clearly established policies and procedures; in response to the need to explain and clarify the rationale and focus of program design; and in response to the need for guidelines for staff who were to continue the development process at Springfield when I left. The organization and presentation of this material in a text is only one small part of the larger process of development and change. Thus, this "final product" represents the work and dedication of the many people who were instrumental in the transformation of program services for patients at Springfield Hospital Center and subsequently at Greystone Park Psychiatric Hospital in New Jersey.

At the Springfield Hospital Center, a sound beginning was possible because of the quality of commitment of Janie Scott, OTR, who had the courage to leave a secure and prestigious setting for the high risk and problems inherent in a large state hospital. Kathy Wassman, RTR, brought a dedication to excellence and provided the critically needed leadership and role modeling for the development of activity therapy. Frederick Pokrass, MD, Superintendent of Springfield, offered the caring and the personal support and understanding that was so crucial to the undertaking. Sandi Malone's objective reflections and technical systems know-how provided the grounding and goal focus that each of us periodically needed. Finally and certainly not least were all the line staff who implemented programs, those who made it really happen, and those other professional and support staff who provided the administration, business, clinical expertise, and the help that was essential for change to occur.

Following my work in Maryland, at the invitation of Oscar Szabadka, Chief Executive Officer, I assumed responsibility for establishing comprehensive rehabilitation services at Greystone Park Psychiatric Hospital. Greystone Park is a large state hospital in New Jersey, which at the time was struggling with a major reorganization and rebuilding of patient services in response to a legal consent agreement that had resulted from a class action suit. Once again, as at Springfield, the building of patient programs required considerable change in the hospital system and in its orientation to patient programs and services. Mr. Szabadka's strong commitment to building quality services at Greystone provided the support that was so essential to change.

Some of the material that had been developed during my work in Maryland was adapted and revised. Because of this earlier experience, it was possible to add to and broaden program design and work toward the development of procedures and policies that would improve the comprehensiveness and integration of services. The work at Greystone also verified that bringing about change in a well-established system is a vigorous undertaking at best. When change is aimed at mainstreaming rehabilitation into a psychiatric hospital, the hurdles become higher.

What was achieved at Greystone was possible because of the commitment and abilities of a number of people. Integrated and collaborative programs among departments became a reality because of the hard work and dedication of Martin Convey, MEd, Director of Education; Irving Bender, MS, OTR, Director of Vocational Rehabilitation; Janice Watson, MS, OTR, Coordinator of Occupational Therapy Services; and Diana Grossweiller, Director of Activity Therapy. Their efforts demonstrated the efficacy of collaborative programs and verified that such sharing serves to more clearly describe the uniqueness of each discipline and enhances services to patients.

In addition, I am indebted to Elyse Rosenblum, MRA, Section Chief, for her unwavering commitment to quality services for patients, her creative intelligence, and the opportunities she created for staff to demonstrate the potential of rehabilitation intervention.

Finally, the breadth of program design, the credibility of assessments, and the relevance of programs for the chronic schizophrenic patients were only some of the contributions of a remarkable occupational therapy staff. I deeply appreciate the contributions of this staff made to the development and refinement of rehabilitation services at Greystone and to the quality of patient care within the larger hospital system; Margaret Allan, OTR; Tara Broderick, MS, OTR; Marilyn Collins, OTR; Iris Lippman, MS, OTR; Amy Kreisberg, OTR; Linda Lidor, MS, OTR; Amy Rotberg, OTR; Harold Sloves, OTR; Betty Soppa, OTR; and Janice Watson, MS, OTR. These acknowledgments would not be complete without a very special thank you to Marie Sheehan, who managed the office and all of us at Greystone with love, firmness, sound organization, humor, and an earthy pragmatism.

Although this book has been developed out of a need for program design in public psychiatric hospitals, much of the content is certainly relevant to the private sector. Likewise, community mental health centers should find some of the material useful, especially those sections that deal with program content and standards. The Standards for Rehabilitation Services in New Jersey's Division of Mental Health and Hospitals, which are based on the material in this book and are reproduced in this work, should be applicable, at least in part, to all mental health systems.

The changes that have occurred in the mental health delivery system and thus in the nature of public hospital populations require an altered perspective regarding treatment interventions. The needs of this population place a priority on services and programs that are directed toward the development and support of those functional skills essential to performing the everyday tasks of living at as independent a level as possible.

This book provides a format, an underlying structure for the design of rehabilitation services in psychiatric hospitals. Its purpose is not to present theory. Rather, it offers a template, a set of guidelines that can be used, in whole or part, in the construction of a system that it is hoped will make the delivery of quality services to patients more likely.

Gail S. Fidler, OTR, FAOTA

1 PURPOSE OF REHABILITATION

The overall purpose of rehabilitation in mental health is to make it possible for the patient to achieve a satisfactory level of functioning in those performance skills that are essential to accomplishing the everyday tasks of living. A satisfactory level of functioning means being able to manage the essential social roles and basic tasks of daily living as independently as possible. It means being able to cope with the demands of one's living environment in ways that are satisfying to one's self and to significant others.

As a process, rehabilitation therefore aims at: (1) improving those physical, psychological, cognitive, and social functions that are fundamental to the acquisition of daily living skills, and (2) providing remedial and new skill learning in relevant self-care, work, and leisure skills. Structurally, rehabilitation services include a number of disciplines, each providing a unique set of specialized services. These services should be organized and offered in a way that ensures a functional continuum directed toward making it possible for the patient to function at the maximum level. Such specialized services most typically include the creative-expressive arts (music, art, dance), education, occupational therapy, physical therapy, recreation, speech and hearing, and vocational rehabilitation.

2 PROGRAM PRINCIPLES

Bachrach (1980) described eight principles that form the basis for effective program design for chronic mental patients. Each of these has a discernible relevance to the organization and delivery of rehabilitation services. Fidler discusses a framework for the structure and focus of remedial programs for the mentally ill (Fidler, 1982). Certain fundamental principles should guide the design and implementation of rehabilitation services. The degree to which programs are effective is determined by the ways in which rehabilitation services operate as integral parts of the hospitals' delivery system, as well as the quality of program content. That is, what kinds of services are provided for the patient? The following principles express both the systems and content requirements for effective programming:

1. *Rehabilitation services must be an integral part of the delivery system in which they operate.* Such services must be assigned a high priority and be viewed as having a value equivalent to the more traditional verbal, clinical therapies. Rehabilitation services must have a functional linkage with the patient care decision-making process in the hospital. Professional quality and expertise must be up to the standards that are set for the traditional clinical professions.

2. *Services must have built-in linkage with resources outside of the hospital.* Rehabilitation services must take responsibility for making such connections an inherent part of programs. It is best to learn and relearn in the environment in which the skill is to be practiced. The structure and operation of services must use community resources as an essential element of programming.

3. *Functional integrity is essential.* Rehabilitation services and departments must be integrated. Shared programs and collaboration in the delivery of services should ensure that the patients' educational, social, physical, psychological, recreational, and vocational needs are addressed in an integrated, developmentally sequential manner.

4. *Program services must be comprehensive.* They must offer a set of services and programs that address, for all patients for whom such needs exist, the following:

- Impairments in sensory organization and processing and in perception.
- Physical debilitation and disabilities.
- Deficiencies in the ability to experience intrinsic gratification and to constructively pursue pleasure.

3

- Impairments in task behaviors and cerebral function.
- Dysfunctions in social and interpersonal behaviors.
- Communication disorders and impairments.
- Limitations in self-care, leisure, and work skills.

5. *Programs must be individualized.* They must ensure a personally tailored regimen that is responsive to the individual needs of the patient and reflects a developmentally sequenced set of learning and remedial experiences congruent with the patient's level of readiness to learn and to integrate an experience.

6. *Services must be organized and structured to provide an environment that is nonthreatening.* Necessary new or remedial learning should be offered in a predictable, consistent manner. The environment should protect against stress and failures, limit chanciness, provide the security of sustained interpersonal support, and reflect the expectation that change and improved function are both expected and possible.

7. *Services must be culturally and economically relevant.* The kind of activities and the environmental context in which they occur must conform to and reflect the cultural and economic realities of the individual patient and the community in which he or she lives or will return to. Activities taught and used must be germane to the individual's past and anticipated life-style and social role. Likewise, program schedules and daily routines should reflect a culturally relevant, normal usage of time, with activities that are appropriate to the particular time of day, week, or year.

8. *A successful service model includes assessment mechanisms or processes that make self-monitoring possible.* Programmatic activities must be regularly measured against the originally established goals and objectives. Services and departments must be clearly linked to the hospital's quality assurance and utilization review programs.

3 PROGRAM PHILOSOPHY AND STRUCTURE

Programming is based on the concept that a sense of competence and social efficacy are fundamental to being able to cope and adapt and that such a sense of self is achieved in large part through successful "doing" experiences that verify achievement, mastery, and social worth.

Acquisition of functional skills is a developmental process and proceeds in a hierarchical manner. Certain sensorimotor, perceptual, cognitive, and psychological behaviors are prerequisites for integrated functions and for the more sophisticated or mature performance skills. Thus, attention must be given to remediating developmental lags or impairments in the areas of sensory, motor, cognitive, psychological, and interpersonal skills before higher order ADL, work, and social skills can be learned. The reparative or habilitative process, especially for the chronic schizophrenic patient, must, insofar as possible, replicate the developmental process of performance skill learning.

Human performance is understood as "the ability to perform those roles and tasks of living that are essential to achieving social efficacy and personal satisfaction" (Fidler, 1982). This encompasses the "ability to care for and maintain oneself at a level of more independence than dependence. It includes the ability to engage in a variety of doing or action experiences that satisfy one's own personal needs and provide intrinsic gratification. It includes finally the ability to make a discernible contribution to the needs and welfare of others" (Fidler, 1982).

Program design in general and individualized services in particular are planned within this context and are focused on those remedial learning experiences that will enable the patient to achieve his or her maximum level of independence in relevant self-care, leisure, and work skills and to achieve an essential balance among these skills. The delivery of services is based on the belief that a patient's ability to respond to and use remedial opportunities is enhanced in a nonthreatening environment. This is an environment that offers structure, predictability, and consistency and that provides freedom, control, feedback, and information processes that are tailored to the needs, capacities, and "readiness" of the individual patient. Programming emphasizes using the patient's existing strengths, skills, and interests as the building blocks to new learning and development.

The types and levels of programs and services provided are based on four central questions:

1. What functional living skills are required or expected of the patient in his or her home environment?

2. In view of such expectations, what functions and dysfunctions exist and at what level?

3. What internal and external factors are impeding the development of essential functions?

4. What remediation or learning is necessary at what levels, and how may existing strengths and resources be used to support and enable the rehabilitation process?

The level and kind of function and dysfunction determine the nature and structure of programs and form the basis for placement in and movement through rehabilitation services. Thus, the design of program services and the regular evaluation of their relevance must be based on data accumulated from an organized, formal instrument used to assess the level of functioning of all patients in the hospital. A variety of such instruments or scales are in use today. The one used in the New Jersey system is reprinted in this book.

Comprehensive, integrated services for patients are the first priority. Collaborative planning among departments must exist in order to design services that respond to the interrelated functional needs of patients. Furthermore, such collaborative efforts make it possible to provide progressive, graded programs, developmentally focused on the acquisition of functional skills for community living.

In accordance with the philosophy of rehabilitation services, the structure and scheduling of programs should reflect the principles of normalization. Both the nature of programs and the times at which they occur must be planned to be congruent with a normal life-style. Thus, evening and weekend hours of recreational activity, library visits, adult education, and the like must be inherent aspects of service. Likewise, special holiday observances on the holiday are an essential component of programming. The use of time, the structure of a day and a week, and the tasks and activities pursued at a given time and in a given environment must reflect what is culturally normal and typical.

4 PROGRAM SERVICES

Rehabilitation services should include the following departments or contracted services in order to provide a continuum of services that will comprise a comprehensive rehabilitation program:

- Activity therapies: including therapeutic recreation and the creative art therapies of movement, art, and music
- Education: including remedial, academic, health, and vocational education
- Occupational therapy
- Physical therapy
- Speech and language, pathology and audiology
- Vocational rehabilitation

The interrelated nature of patients' varied rehabilitation needs makes some role overlap among departments inevitable and desirable. Roles assigned to a department or a given staff must always be based on the disciplines and/or the individual staff's professional preparation to provide such service. Role definition for any given department or service cannot routinely be made on the basis of the modalities used. Rather, role description and differentiation is based on why and how a modality is used.

There are both generic and specialized discipline-specific roles and functions. A successful rehabilitation model recognizes both differences and commonalities and by design ensures that the specialized needs of the patient will receive expert attention. It defines generic functions and appropriate role overlapping in order to maximize the availability of services to a patient and to coordinate those services. When rehabilitation services are designed solely around a generic or transdisciplinary model, the patients are too often deprived of the *specialized* services that are essential and programs are not cost-effective because of misuse of expert staff. The following goals and objectives define the primary roles that should be expected of each of the rehabilitation departments or services.

ACTIVITY THERAPY

Goals

To provide a variety of therapeutic recreation, sports, arts, crafts, dance, games, music, and library activities commensurate with patient needs, interests, and culture for the purpose of:

1. Stimulating, developing, and reinforcing interests and healthy action patterns;

2. Meeting individual needs for achievement, acceptance, expression, self-direction, creativity, pleasure, and physical well-being;

3. Providing opportunities to learn leisure-time skills and to achieve a level of interest and skill adequate to sustain the desire to use leisure time constructively;

4. Reinforcing and providing practice in social behaviors; and

5. Creating an environment that supports the sense of personal worth, competence, and efficacy.

Objectives

1. Develop social relationships.
2. Increase comfort in social situations.
3. Explore activity interests.
4. Learn and practice leisure skills.
5. Increase awareness of and responsiveness to the outside world.
6. Experience pleasure in play.
7. Engage in creative expression.
8. Explore various modes of communication.
9. Improve gait coordination and posture.
10. Improve body balance and coordination.
11. Increase frustration tolerance.
12. Manage competition.
13. Increase energy output.
14. Reduce hyperactivity.
15. Improve muscle tone and physical fitness.
16. Practice cooperative group member skills.

EDUCATION

Goals

1. To provide an individually appropriate academic education program that is adapted to the capacities and needs of the patient and designed to maintain the patient's educational and intellectual development;

2. To offer special, individually designed, remedial education experiences in order to diminish learning deficits and reduce learning problems;

3. To provide specially designed and structured learning experiences to stimulate awareness of and/or teach vocational skills, social skills and behaviors; health maintaining behaviors and habits; disease prevention; disease, and cultural and civic interests.

4. To generate and reinforce positive expectations about learning and achievement.

Objectives

1. Improve motivation to learn.
2. Increase and expand interests.
3. Improve cognitive functions.
4. Increase attention span.
5. Explore new interests.
6. Increase social comfort and skills.
7. Expand knowledge.
8. Engage in creative expression.
9. Increase knowledge of self.
10. Increase knowledge of health and of health issues.
11. Complete grade requirements.
12. Learn specific vocational skills.
13. Explore vocational interests.
14. Improve communication skills.
15. Master fundamental reading, math, and writing skills.
16. Practice group participation skills.
17. Experience success.
18. Cope with failure and with competition.
19. Clarify values and attitudes.

OCCUPATIONAL THERAPY

Goals

1. To create a performance skill learning and practice environment with sufficient regularity, predictability, continuity, reinforcement, and feedback so that essential coping and survival skills become habitual patterns of behavior;

2. To provide acting-doing experiences that will enable the patient to acquire a repertoire of self-care, work, and leisure-time skills sufficient for achieving a maximum level of independence, developing a life-style more appropriate to the social and cultural role expectations of the individual's society. and experiencing a sense of self-satisfaction and personal worth.

3. To alter the role orientation from passive recipient to self agent, to develop a sense of being able to influence and have some control over one's daily life; and

4. To reduce dependency on external motivating forces and increase self-initiating behaviors.

Objectives

1. Describe the nature and level of each patient's skills and deficits in sensorimotor integration, physical functions, task behaviors, interpersonal and group skills, and leisure-time patterns and skills.

2. Offer task and activity experiences matched to individual needs and capacities that will:

   a. Provide the required sensorimotor stimulation and physical restoration to enhance the ability to receive, organize, and respond to stimuli; facilitate normal movement; increase muscle strength and endurance; improve dexterity and coordination; increase energy level; and improve attention span.

   b. Improve task performance behaviors and diminish cognitive disorganization;

   c. Teach self-maintenance skills and activities of daily living so that the patient is able to care for and maintain the self at a more independent level; and

   d. Teach those habits, attitudes, and skills that comprise the cognitive tasks and interpersonal behaviors required for sheltered or competitive employment and/or for being able to make some discernible contribution to the needs and welfare of others.

3. Teach and reinforce those interpersonal and social skills that are essential for establishing reciprocally satisfying relationships with others.

More specifically, occupational therapy programming includes, at levels commensurate with the patient's functional abilities and skill-learning needs and readiness, those individual and group tasks and activity experiences that may include, but are not necessarily limited to, the following performance components (Fidler, 1982):

Sensorimotor Integration
- Balance and equilibrium
- Occular control and visual perception
- Tactile discrimination
- Bilateral motor coordination
- Visual-motor integration
- Language and auditory skills
- Gross motor coordination and mobility
- Fine motor coordination and dexterity
- Muscle strength and endurance
- Work tolerance

Self-Maintenance
- Personal hygiene and grooming
- Meal planning
- Money management
- Shopping skills
- Eating habits and cooking skills
- Use of public transportation
- Housekeeping and home management skills
- Time management
- Self-protection and handling emergencies
- Initial encounter skills
- Conversational skills
- Table manners and eating-out behavior
- Telephoning
- Interactive skills: giving, sharing, receiving
- Eliciting positive response
- Making friends
- Assertive behavior skills
- Group participation and cooperative skills
- Responding: giving, receiving, and using feedback
- Perceiving and appropriately responding to differences in social role expectations; interpersonal contacts

Task Behaviors
- Time management
- Goal setting
- Goal directedness
- Reality orientation
- Cause and effect awareness
- Fine and/or gross motor skills
- Work tolerance, endurance
- Attention span, directing energy
- Task organization, sequencing
- Self-appraisal skills
- Handling job stress
- Coping with success, failure, competition
- Negotiating co-worker relationships
- Workmanship
- Handling supervision, direction, orders
- Decision making
- Learning specific work and job related skills

Leisure Skills
- Exploring interests and abilities
- Learning and practicing leisure activities
- Planning, organizing, and using non-work time
- Knowing and pursuing self-gratifying activity
- Exploring and using at-home community resources
- Knowing and using activities to do alone and with others

VOCATIONAL REHABILITATION

Goals

To provide an actual work practice and work skills learning environment that will, in accordance with patient needs:

1. Support the integration of those work attitudes and habits that are fundamental to work readiness;

2. Teach and reinforce work behaviors so that time management, workmanship, attention span, organization, work tolerance, and dependability reach a level that is adequate for sheltered or competitive employment or vocational training;

3. Provide learning and practice in those interpersonal behaviors that comprise essential worker relationship skills;

4. Offer opportunities to explore and reinforce work interests, aptitudes, and skills; and

5. Teach work skills and provide the opportunity and guidance to apply these to the demands and realities of the work world.

Objectives

1. Increase work tolerance and endurance.
2. Improve time management.
3. Increase attention span.
4. Enhance workmanship expectations.
5. Improve work incentive.
6. Enhance perception of cause and effect.
7. Increase dependability, reliability.
8. Improve self-reliance.
9. Improve management of time pressures.
10. Increase ability to handle supervision and direction and negotiate worker relationships.
11. Learn self-appraisal and accountability skills.
12. Learn workmanship skills.
13. Objectify self-other expectations.
14. Explore work interests and abilities.
15. Use, develop, and/or maintain specific job skills.

PHYSICAL THERAPY

Goals

1. To apply modalities of heat, light, massage, radial energy, sound, and exercise to correct or reduce a physical disability or impairment, minimize or prevent debilitation, and increase neuromotor alertness;

2. To evaluate and assess muscle and joint functions, mobility, body structure, and function;

3. To provide instruction and training in the use of prosthetic, orthotic, and other assistive devices;

4. To provide consultation and advisory services to reduce incident of disability, body malfunction, and pain; and

5. To fit and adapt braces, splints, wheelchairs, walkers, crutches, and other devices to improve function and mobility and decrease deformity.

Objectives

1. Increase muscle tone.
2. Increase range of motion.
3. Improve gait and mobility.
4. Teach transfer techniques.
5. Increase muscle strength and endurance.
6. Improve functional use of extremities.
7. Increase neuromotor alertness and response.
8. Improve body positioning and coordination.
9. Minimize debilitation.
10. Teach energy conservation, joint protection.
11. Teach cane, walker, crutch, and wheelchair use and management.

SPEECH AND LANGUAGE PATHOLOGY AND AUDIOLOGY

Goals

1. To conduct or provide screening tests and assessments in speech, language, and hearing in order to identify and describe hearing impairments and communication disorders;

2. To provide remedial programs for the development of language and communication skills; and

3. To provide auditory training and to teach the use of manual and/or electronic communication devices.

Objectives

1. Improve articulation, vocalization, muscle tone, and control.

2. Develop prelinguistic skills and receptive and expressive language skills.

3. Increase comprehension of the speech of others.

4. Improve ability to communicate with others.

5. Increase comfort in communicating with others.

6. Teach use of communication aids and devices and sign language.

7. Provide opportunities for the practice of communicating with others.

5 STAFFING AND SUPERVISORY PATTERNS

Staffing patterns and staff ratios will depend mainly on the nature of the patient population and the organizational structure of the hospital or center. For example, if there are many geriatric patients, the need for physical therapists, speech and language pathologists, and occupational therapists will be greater than for vocational rehabilitation or remedial education staff.

Supervisory patterns, the particular roles and duties assigned to staff, and other unique factors in a given setting will influence how staffing ratios are set. Ideally, nonsupervisory staff should spend 60% of their time in direct patient care and approximately 40% in support services. With supervisory responsibilities, direct care time is, of course, reduced, and additional staff may be needed to meet the patients' direct service care needs. Direct patient care time is time spent in contact with patients. It does not include treatment team meetings (unless the patient is present) nor does it include supervisory or documentation time. Considering all the variables, the following formulas are a guide for estimating staffing needs for each of the services:

Activity Therapy Staff: 1 Staff Person to Every 22 Patients in the Hospital. This ratio makes it possible to comply with JCAH standards for evening, weekend, and holiday recreational and social activities for all patients. The composition of the staff—that is, the apportionment of recreation, movement, music, and art positions—will depend on the nature of the patient population and the recruitment realities in the area. However, hiring staff whose basic education enables them to offer a variety of services and modalities is cost-effective. The nature of the public hospital system and population and the need for broad recreational and social experiences makes it important to have an activity therapy staff with training and experience in therapeutic recreation.

A ratio of four paraprofessionals to one professional in activity therapy should not be exceeded. Adequate supervision and quality programming is difficult if the ratio is higher.

Occupational Therapy Staff: 1 Staff Person to Every 25 Patients in the Hospital. Certified occupational therapy assistants can make up part of this staff complement. However, the ratio of two assistants for each professional occupational therapist should not be exceeded. If certified occupational therapy assistants are not available, then a ratio of one aide to one professional applies. It is critical that there be enough professional occupational therapists to cover all treatment teams.

17

Considering the characteristically varied population of psychiatric hospitals, professional occupational therapy staff should be a hiring priority. The occupational therapist is educated to provide a full continuum of services, spanning the rehabilitation spectrum from the fundamental level of sensorimotor organization and physical dysfunction to task behaviors, ADL, and pre-vocational and work skills.

Staffing in physical therapy, vocational rehabilitation, speech and hearing, and education should be determined by the number of hospital patients who are identified as having a physical disability or a physically debilitating illness, communication problems and impairments, or deficits in educational, learning, and/or vocational skills. These data should then be assessed in terms of the approximate number of patients who, with specialized services, can be expected to respond positively—that is, those who show improvement in terms of diminution of the specified disability or deficit.

Generally, in a public hospital, a maximum of 35% of the patient population will require vocational rehabilitation programming and educational services, and 20% of the long-term population of a public hospital will require physical therapy. Approximately 15% of this patient population will require speech and language therapy.

Some neurological and physical impairments and dysfunctions are irreversible due to their chronicity or etiology: sometimes the potential for improvement is so minimal that prolonged, specialized treatment is not helpful to the patient or cost-effective for the system. In such instances, resources are better used to help the patient adapt and adjust to the disability and learn compensatory and splinter skills that will improve overall functioning and enhance the quality of the patient's life. Such adaptive programs are generally inappropriate priorities for such specialized services as physical therapy, education, speech and hearing, or vocational rehabilitation. Since the occupational therapist is trained to work with the most dysfunctional patients, programs focused on compensatory or splinter skill learning are more appropriately and efficiently managed by occupational therapy in collaboration with the activity therapies.

A minimal staffing formula for the more specialized services may be:

• *Speech and Language Pathology and Audiology:* One professional for every 25 patients requiring speech and communication remediation.

• *Education:* One certified teacher for every 11 patients who are 21 years of age or younger. One teacher/instructor for every 25 adult patients requiring education services.

• *Vocational Rehabilitation:* One staff person for every 20 patients requiring vocational rehabilitation services. A ratio of two for each professional is acceptable. When a compensated/sheltered workshop is operated as part of program services, technical staff will be required to manage the necessary support services related to contract management and to CARF standards.

• *Physical Therapy:* One physical therapist for every 30 patients who require physical therapy services. Two physical therapy assistants to each professional should not be exceeded.

6 PROGRAM ORGANIZATION AND OPERATIONS

Organization of rehabilitation services will reflect the organizational and operational patterns of the hospital. However, several factors are critical to cost-effective, high-quality services.

Organizational structure must reflect and support the principles of integrated, comprehensive rehabilitation services and the priority of these services in the spectrum of patient care and treatment. In each division or unit of the large hospital, a rehabilitation services professional should be responsible for coordinating rehabilitation services within that area and functioning as the liaison and resource to other disciplines and treatment teams. Such responsibility includes ensuring the integration and coordination of rehabilitation services and carrying administrative responsibility for all rehabilitation staff assigned to that unit or service area. This coordinator/supervisor should be a senior professional with experience and education in the full spectrum of rehabilitation service needs (i.e., physical disabilities, sensory integration, ADL, prevocational training, work, and leisure). Such a supervisor should also be expected to provide some direct patient care services.

There is continuous debate about the relative merits of a decentralized hospital structure as compared to a centralized model. Administrative staff most frequently support a decentralized system with relatively autonomous sections or divisions. Professional services staff usually favor a centralized model with relatively autonomous departments accountable to a professional department head who is generally responsible to a clinical director. Experience indicates that advantages and disadvantages exist in each and that the best system will combine the strengths of both, thus reducing the problems and pitfalls.

A decentralized structure is valuable because it makes accountability clear. It enables the section chief to control staffing assignments and programmatic operations, thus eliminating the problem of the section chief's being responsible for the division but having no control over staff assignments or schedules. With staff directly responsible to the section chief, communication and collaboration with a department head is less critical for the section chief. The complexities of having to negotiate power and leverage with a variety of department heads is essentially eliminated. For the line staff, a decentralized system means being responsible and accountable to only one boss.

On the other hand, centralized departments are more cost-effective and more responsive to professional standards. Program standards and role delineations are best defined and monitored by the relevant profession. This is an extremely important factor, because the function of departments within rehabilitation services is frequently not well-understood by hospital staff. Without centralized control and monitoring, such services are frequently at risk of being defined as an adjunctive service to the psychotherapies or otherwise misperceived and underutilized.

Centralized services make it possible to deploy resources when and where they are needed, thus reducing costly duplication of equipment and staff. The cost-effectiveness of centralizing specialized programs such as physical therapy, vocational rehabilitation, and education is reasonably clear. A centralized organizational structure for activity therapy and occupational therapy is no less rational, but it should not preclude staff's being assigned responsibility for a specific patient population on a given unit. Such responsibility must include obligations for sustained communication and collaboration with the professional and administrative staff of the unit or division as well as a clear accountability for responding to the program needs of the unit.

Effective management and service delivery in a centralized structure requires skillful communication and collaboration, but, most important, it requires a clear understanding on the part of the department head of what services that department should and can provide to a given unit or division. The division or unit chief and the department head in essence negotiate a service contract. The "contract" is arrived at on the basis of the divisions' specified needs for service and the departments' ability to provide a given service for a specific period of time. Such agreements are reviewed and renegotiated whenever there is a structural change in the system or alterations in the patient population. Otherwise, review and redevelopment of a contract should be done annually. Such contracts must be clear and specific in regard to the assignment of staff as well as the kind and frequency of services. It must be understood that changes in any aspect of the contract will be made only by agreement between the unit or section chief and the department head.

The programming in occupational therapy and activity therapy that is required for all patients in a hospital makes it essential that such staff have permanent assignments to a given unit or division. This ensures consistency and continuity in programming and in treatment team participation, collaboration, and communication. Staff must always be responsive to the division head for providing relevant, quality programs and responsible to the rehabilitation coordinator. Collaboration between the rehabilitation program coordinator and the division head is critical in the design and monitoring of programs as well as in staff evaluations, hiring, and placement. Both the formal and informal operating procedures of the hospital must provide for and support such collaboration. Table 1 summarizes the shared and separate responsibilities of the division chief and the department head.

20

Table 1. Responsibilities of Section Chief and Department Head

Section Chief's Responsibilities	Shared Responsibilities	Department Head's Responsibilities
Manage the milieu of the division.	Program design and evaluation: needs assessment, identification of program purpose, priority of program need, program design, identification of the resources needed and available.	Interpret and monitor professional standards.
Administer allocated resources: fiscal, facilities, staff.	Program scheduling.	Provide professional guidance and supervision to staff.
Manage the ongoing delivery of contracted services.	Ongoing monitoring of service contract and program quality.	Describe the components of services which can be offered by the department.
Monitor and ensure quality of patient care.	Allocation and assignment of staff and their responsibilities.	Participate in development and implementation of training and education (Inservice, conferences, continuing education, graduate study, and internships).
Manage patient flow: admissions and discharges.	Staff evaluations, EPEIS, dual signatures.	Stimulate, develop, and monitor research efforts, special projects, and grants.
Administer and facilitate the treatment team process.	Hiring, firing, and promoting of staff and disciplinary actions.	Assure the quality of services.
Initiate and maintain a process for coordinating all programs and services in the division.		Recruit and screen staff.
		Provide specialized expertise to treatment teams, other staff, and programs.

Close working relationships between rehabilitation services and the clinical services are critical. The success of programming is shaped by the nature of these relationships, the formal and informal communication patterns, and the mutual understanding and respect among staffs. It is essential that department heads from each discipline meet regularly to facilitate collaborative planning, program sharing, support, and mutual problem solving. The relationship between the directors of the clinical and rehabilitation departments should model the collaboration and mutual respect expected of all staff.

The treatment team is a significant force in the treatment and rehabilitation process. Ideally, all staff involved with the patient should contribute to the team's planning and treatment review process. This may be impractical, however, because of limited staff, especially professionals, and the priority of direct patient service. The role of the unit-based rehabilitation coordinator thus becomes essential to ensure feedback to and communication with the treatment team and to facilitate the referral process.

In order to meet the requirement for evening, weekend, and holiday programs, staff hours must be arranged so that such services are possible and so that special "evening only" staffing is avoided. Having an evening and weekend shift to provide program for patients creates a class of "second-rate" staff who are removed from the mainstream of patient treatment and the related feedback and communication process. It is preferable to develop staff schedules that make it possible for the staff to work some days, some evenings, some weekends, and some holidays.

Although it is expected that the recreational therapist will bring the highest level of expertise to leisure-time programming, it is also expected that other disciplines in rehabilitation services will contribute to evening, weekend, and holiday programming. Occupational therapy, adult education, creative arts therapy, vocational counseling groups for working patients, and speech and communication clubs are some of the programs, in addition to recreation, that should comprise evening and weekend activities for patients. Policies and procedures for developing and maintaining well-planned special holiday programs are essential. Such policies should specify:

• The procedures for planning, organizing, and implementing holiday programs;

• The number or percentage of staff people required for each holiday;

• A system (e.g., rotation schedule) for determining staff holiday assignments well in advance of the holiday;

• A list of holidays to be observed (Programming should be available for each holiday, but there may be holidays for which other departments or services, such as volunteers, chaplain, or nursing or food services, assume responsibility.); and

• The procedure for obtaining equivalent time or other means of compensating for a holiday on duty.

It is essential that adequate supervision be provided and that supervisory level staff be on site at all times when programs are offered on holidays, evenings, and weekends.

Programmatic and administrative collaborative planning and decision making among the rehabilitation departments is crucial. There is seldom an issue or concern that affects only one department. Therefore, regular meetings of department heads should be held for the purposes of:

• Reviewing and critiquing both the program quality and the relevance of programs to the patient population based on a level of function data collection;

• Reviewing indicated needs for change and making decisions relative to changes;

• Generating special programs, projects, and grants;

• Setting goals and time frames for changes and goal achievement;

• Establishing and reviewing departmental roles and functions;

• Establishing and reviewing program standards and policies;

• Establishing and reviewing practice standards and policies;

• Reviewing and dealing with staff needs and personnel problems;

• Reviewing, coordinating, and establishing student internship programs;

• Monitoring and making decisions relative to budgetary planning, expenditures, allocations, and use of facilities;

• Reviewing and making decisions regarding departmental relationships and liaisons with other departments and programs within the hospital and in the outside community; and

• Providing opportunities for sharing ideas and perspectives and for creative planning and innovative use of resources.

In addition, *department heads* should meet with their staff on a weekly basis for purposes of:

• Ensuring that program content is relevant to patient needs;

• Ensuring that scheduling is coordinated with other activities and services on the unit;

• Providing guidance and counseling to staff;

• Monitoring documentation of services;

• Reviewing referrals and the referral process;

• Identifying staff education needs;

• Developing and monitoring student programs;

• Providing feedback about and discussion of departmental and hospital matters and business;

• Developing special projects, research, and grants; and

• Supporting and enhancing communication, collaboration, and creative planning.

Regularly scheduled individual supervision should be provided for new, inexperienced staff and available to other staff as necessary.

Figures 1 and 2 reflect two somewhat different patterns of organization and lines of authority. Figure 1 shows the director of rehabilitation services being responsible to the clinical director. There are three associate directors of rehabilitation services—one for vocational adjustment, one for occupational therapy, and one for activity therapy. These three associate directors report to the director of rehabilitation services. The associate directors for occupational therapy and activity therapy services coordinate and collaborate with the division supervisors, who in turn are responsible for supervising staff and delivering services to each of the divisions.

In Figure 2 the director of rehabilitation services is responsible to the chief executive officers of the hospital and has a line relationship with the clinical director. Six department heads report to the director of rehabilitation services, and these department heads have line relationships with the department heads in clinical services.

The unit-based rehabilitation program coordinators report to the director of occupational therapy and in turn supervise the occupational therapy and activity therapy staff who are assigned to the unit. The rehabilitation program coordinators direct all rehabilitation services on the unit and represent rehabilitation services on the treatment teams of the unit. The director of activity therapy functions as a resource to the director of occupational therapy and the unit-based coordinators in terms of activity therapy services on these units. In addition, this director is responsible for all centralized leisure-time programs. The activity therapy unit-based staff are directly responsible to the director of activity therapy for 12 hours a week of centralized recreation services.

Figure 3 shows the functional linkage between departments as well as the unique programmatic responsibilities of each department. Speech and hearing and education collaborate in planning and providing programs that are related to manual communication and remedial learning needs. Education and vocational rehabilitation share responsibility for the development of vocational education programs and services. Occupational and vocational rehabilitation work together in prevocational programs. Education and occupational therapy share programs and collaborate in relation to perceptual motor training and special programs for the learning disabled. Physical therapy, speech, and occupational therapy collaborate in programs of feeding, communication, and positioning. Occupational therapy and activity therapy share in designing and implementing leisure skill programs, and occupational therapy and physical therapy collaborate and share programs in physical restoration and orthotics as well as programs to improve gross motor skills and range of motion.

Figure 1

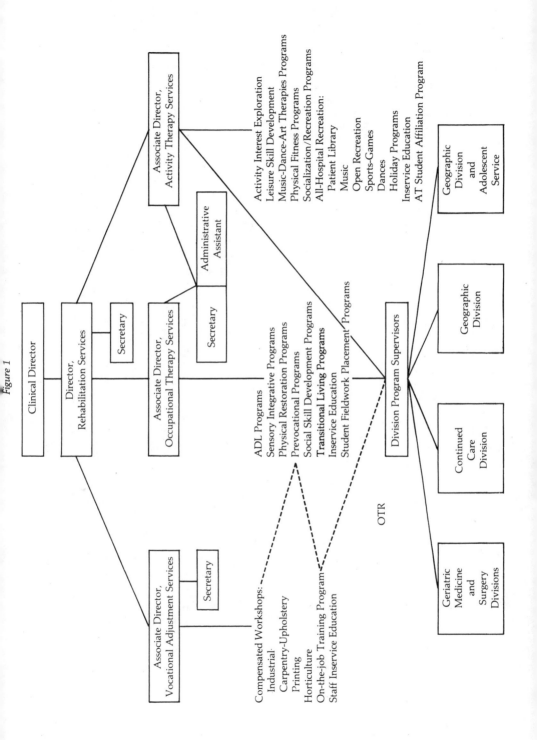

25

Figure 2

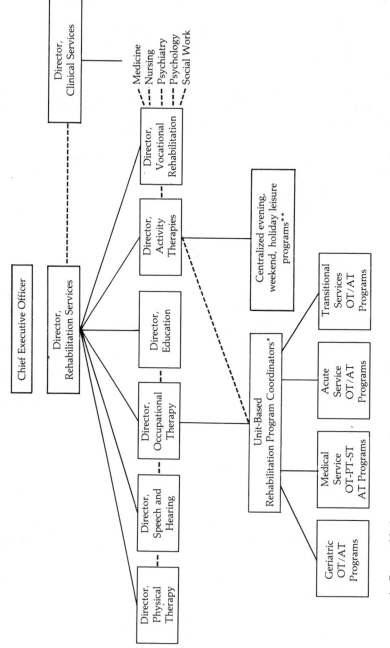

* Responsible for representing and/or assuring rehabilitation services on representation or input to treatment teams;
  • Facilitating referral process;
  • Planning coordination unit-based OT/AT programs;
  • Clinical supervision of staff as appropriate;
  • Liaison with section chief and staff; and
  • Ensuring liaison with other rehabilitation departments and services.

** Unit-based AT staff responsible to and accountable to AT director for 12 hours weekly for centralized programs.

Figure 3

Functional Linkage and Program Responsibilities

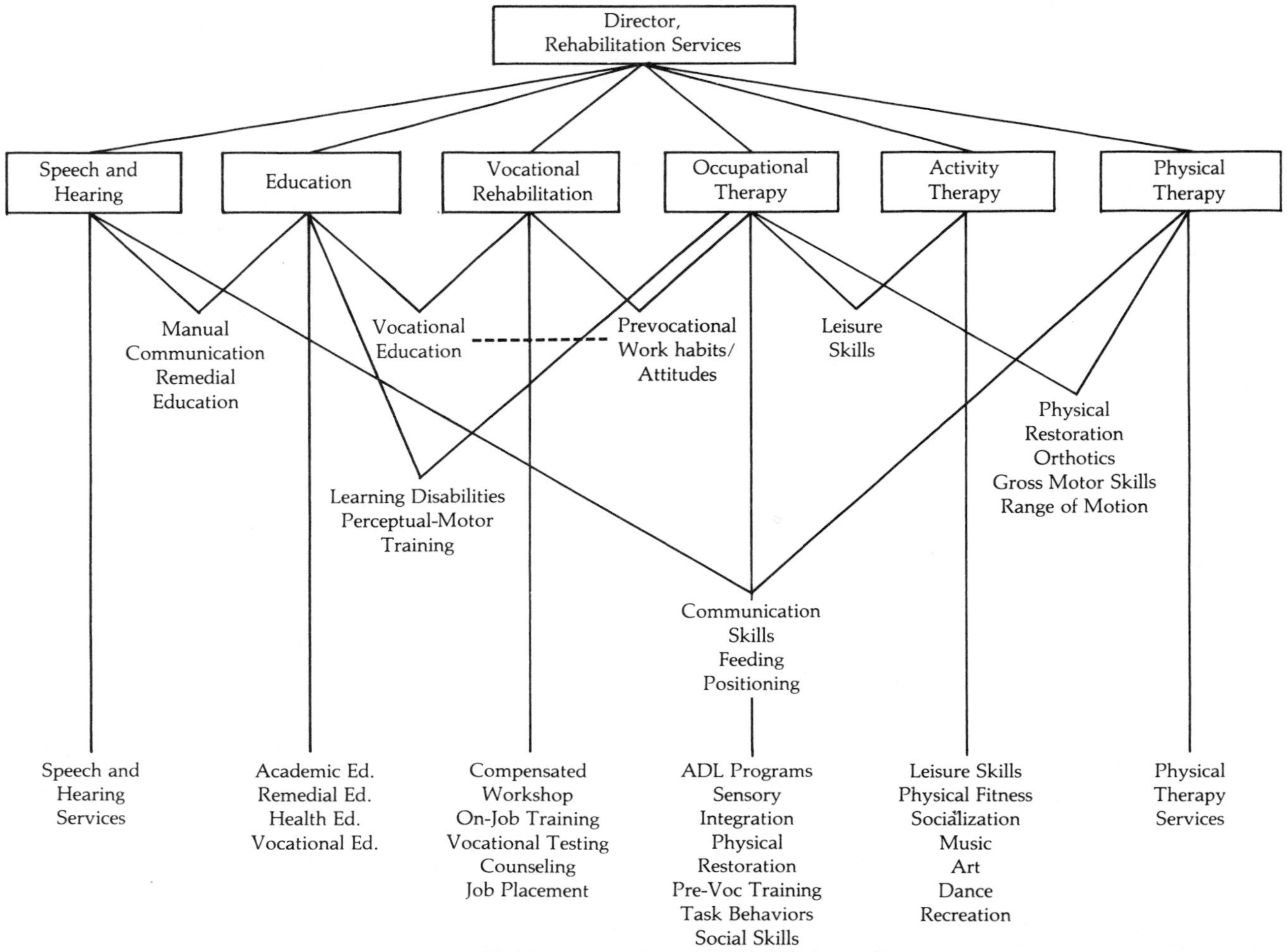

Director, Rehabilitation Services

Speech and Hearing

Education

Vocational Rehabilitation

Occupational Therapy

Activity Therapy

Physical Therapy

Manual Communication
Remedial Education

Learning Disabilities
Perceptual-Motor Training

Vocational Education

Prevocational Work habits/Attitudes

Leisure Skills

Physical Restoration
Orthotics
Gross Motor Skills
Range of Motion

Speech and Hearing Services

Academic Ed.
Remedial Ed.
Health Ed.
Vocational Ed.

Compensated Workshop
On-Job Training
Vocational Testing
Counseling
Job Placement

ADL Programs
Sensory Integration
Physical Restoration
Pre-Voc Training
Task Behaviors
Social Skills

Communication Skills
Feeding
Positioning

Leisure Skills
Physical Fitness
Socialization
Music
Art
Dance
Recreation

Physical Therapy Services

27

7 REFERRALS

Guiding the treatment teams toward the most productive and appropriate use of rehabilitation services is an ongoing concern. It is seldom possible to have a rehabilitation services representative always available to all teams for all treatment planning sessions. Furthermore, it is not always possible to have a representative who is fully knowledgeable about all service aspects of each department. Guides for referrals to the various services are helpful to the treatment teams and also serve to educate staff about each service and its role in patient care. These guides for referrals are made available to each treatment team member and are used to help staff make appropriate referrals.

GUIDE FOR REFERRAL TO ACTIVITY THERAPY

The following represent those areas of patient needs that can be filled by activity therapy programming. A referral should specify one or more of these areas when individualized treatment is indicated. (All patients may participate in open recreation groups and social activities, which do not require a referral.)

- Developing social relationships;
- Increasing comfort in social situations;
- Exploring activity interests;
- Learning and practicing leisure skills;
- Stimulating awareness of and responsiveness to the outside world;
- Experiencing pleasure in play;
- Providing creative expression;
- Improving gait coordination and posture;
- Improving body balance and coordination;
- Increasing frustration tolerance;
- Managing competition;
- Increasing energy output;
- Reducing hyperactivity;
- Participating in cooperative group endeavor.

GUIDE FOR REFERRAL TO OCCUPATIONAL THERAPY

The following represent components of functioning or elements of behavior related to performance skills (AOTA, 1979). When one or more of these exist as a problem or learning need, a referral to occupational therapy is indicated. A referral should specify a problem, a learning need, or a need for assessment in one or more of the following:

• *Self-Care/Self-Maintenance Skills*—Performance of daily personal care, which includes grooming, eating, dressing, functional mobility, use of public transportation, use of the telephone, care of personal belongings, single meal preparation, money management, and care of living space.

• *Work Skills*—Work attitudes and habits, task organization, prevocational and prework training, household management, time management, and work tolerance.

• *Leisure Skills*—Constructive, pleasurable use of non-work time, leisure interests, relaxation, self-expression, and leisure skills development.

• *Sensorimotor Behaviors*—Range of motion, gross and fine motor coordination, sensory awareness, visual-spatial awareness, body integration, muscle strength, and endurance and mobility.

• *Cognition*—Performance in comprehending, defining, and adjusting oneself with regard to time, place, and person; orientation, concentration sequencing, memory, and perceiving casual relationships.

• *Therapeutic Adaptations*—Application and use of splints, braces, and slings to improve performance, decrease deformity; wheelchair management and positioning.

• *Psychologic Functions*—Frustration tolerance, coping with fear and anxiety, modifying behavior, setting realistic goals, accepting responsibility for self, differentiating self from others, self-expectations, and managing successes and failures.

• *Social Skills*—Peer relationships, coping with authority, group interactional skills, responsiveness to others, collaborative, interdependent relationship skills, giving, receiving, and sharing.

GUIDE FOR REFERRAL TO VOCATIONAL REHABILITATION

Patients being referred to this service are expected to be able to function at an intermediate or moderate skill level with regard to cognitive orientation and organization, concentration, attention span, memory, motor coordination, mobility, self-control, personal hygiene, and toileting. Generally, this includes:

• Ability to concentrate on an organized task for at least one-half hour without a break.

• Ability to follow instructions without close supervision.

• Capacity to sustain a regular work schedule of four half days per week.

• A level of functioning (LOF) scale rating at level 3 or above in all categories except for personal care skills.

• An LOF scale rating at level 4 in the personal care skills category.

The following represent those areas of performance skill learning, practice, and assessment that can be responded to by the vocational rehabilitation department. A referral should specify one or more of these skill development areas.

• Explore work interests, aptitudes, and skills;
• Develop work interests and incentives;
• Maintain prior work skills;
• Focus existing skills, interests, and ability;
• Improve work tolerance and endurance;
• Develop specific workmanship skills and standards;
• Provide structure and focus for work incentive or work ethic;
• Learn time management, order, and organization;
• Learn job-related dependability, reliability, and self-reliance;
• Improve task organization and task sequencing;
• Learn cause-and-effect relationships;
• Experience work success and approval from others;
• Practice negotiating co-worker relationships;
• Improve ability to accept worker role, subjugate personal preferences to job demands;
• Improve ability to cope with and manage supervision and direction;
• Develop more realistic self-appraisal in work setting;
• Increase tolerance for work-related constraints and pressures.

GUIDE FOR REFERRAL TO EDUCATION

The following represent those learning needs that can be met by an education program. A referral to education should specify one or more of these areas of focus:

- Improving motivation to learn;
- Increasing and expanding educational interests;
- Improving reading, math, and writing skills;
- Increasing knowledge of health and health-related issues;
- Completing grade requirements;
- Exploring vocational interests;
- Improving communication skills;
- Experiencing success in learning;
- Practicing group participation skills;
- Coping with failure and competition;
- Engaging in creative expression;
- Stimulating intellectual development;
- Pursuing a topic of special interest.

GUIDE FOR REFERRAL TO SPEECH AND HEARING SERVICES

When one or more of the following communication problems are evident or in question, a referral to the speech and hearing service should be made.

- Articulating and vocalizing;
- Hearing and comprehending the speech of others;
- Communicating with others;
- Hearing and distinguishing sounds;
- Using manual communication;
- Using auditory and communication devices.

GUIDE FOR REFERRAL TO PHYSICAL THERAPY

A referral to physical therapy is indicated when one or more of the following problems is evident.

- Limitations in the range of motion or muscle strength and/or tone;
- Difficulties in ambulation and balance;
- Muscle weakness, fatigue, and/or debilitation;
- Joint stiffness or immobility;
- Contractures;
- Difficulties in wheelchair management and positioning;
- Difficulties in management of crutch or walker;
- Need for orthopedic, prosthetic, and adaptive equipment.

8 EVALUATIONS AND ASSESSMENTS

Patient evaluations and assessments are the basis on which individualized rehabilitation goals are developed. They provide the data that make it possible to set priorities from among several rehabilitation goals, and they are the yardstick for monitoring progress and planning for discharge.

An initial rehabilitation needs assessment should be completed as early as possible for all patients admitted to the hospital. This initial assessment provides an overview of the patient's functional skills and performance history. The information should be used by the treatment team to formulate a treatment plan and to set priorities. The assessment should make it possible to specify to which rehabilitation services referrals should be made and in which areas there is a need for additional, in-depth evaluation. This initial assessment should include data regarding the following:

- *Education*—current and past interests, abilities, and achievements.
- *Work history*—history of past employment and work experiences, current work skills, interests, attitudes, and abilities.
- *Leisure skills*—current and past leisure interests and abilities, leisure patterns, pursuits, and skills.
- *Physical functioning*—posture, gait, coordination, or mobility disabilities and limitations; hearing, speech, and/or visual limitations.
- *Social*—interpersonal attitudes, characteristic social behaviors, group skills, friendships, and family relationships.
- *Self-care and self-maintenance skills*—daily personal care skills, self-care, care of personal belongings and living space.
- *Life-style*—daily activity patterns, daily time use.
- *Recommendations*—for rehabilitation focus, special interventions, and referrals for services and/or further evaluations.

Some of the information that is needed for an initial rehabilitation assessment is frequently available in the social history, and there is no need to duplicate data gathering if material is already available. It is important, however, to interview the patient and obtain the patient's perspective on the material at hand as well as to gather other or additional information. Keep in mind that the purpose of gathering data at this stage is to obtain an overview of the patient's strengths and deficits in managing the tasks of his or her everyday world. Such a configuration includes information from a variety of sources, arranged in such a way as to provide a perspective with regard to performance patterns and those related functional deficits that impair coping and adaptation. One such evaluative instrument is Black's Adolescent Role Assessment (Black, 1976). This assessment puts together a configuration comprised of performance patterns and attitudes regarding childhood play, adolescent socialization in school and with family and peers, occupational choices and work attitudes, and goals. The Life Style Performance Profile (Fidler, 1982) attempts to get at such perspectives for the adult population. Both instruments are very useful in developing an initial rehabilitation assessment. The Life Style Performance Profile is reprinted in the Appendix.

There are a variety of activity interest checklists and activity assessments. The Greystone Park Psychiatric Hospital Activity Interest Profile is an example of an extremely simple instrument that has been used to obtain information on activity interest from a long-term patient population. The information that is gathered from this profile is used to plan leisure-time programs and is updated on a yearly basis (see Appendix).

The Ancora Psychiatric Hospital Activities Assessment is a more thorough, complex instrument. It provides a profile of the individual patient's interests and use of leisure time and the physical, social, and psychological factors affecting activity (see Appendix).

In a large public psychiatric hospital, the Parachek Rating Scale for geriatric patients is a cost-effective and useful instrument (Parachek, 1976). This instrument provides a simple rating scale that makes program design and patient placement in programs a relatively simple and effective process. One of the marked values of this instrument is that it involves both nursing and occupational therapy staff in shared assessment processes. Thus, collaboration and program commitment are frequently natural outcomes. The rating scale also provides an easy, valid way of documenting progress over a sustained period of time, an important factor in long-term patient care.

When a patient is referred to occupational therapy, an occupational therapy assessment is to be completed and should include, as appropriate to the referral, an in-depth assessment of:

- Sensorimotor integration and perception;
- Physical functioning;
- Task behaviors and cognitive skills;
- Self-maintenance skills and limitations;
- Interpersonal and group skills and behaviors;
- Leisure interests and patterns;
- Activity configuration summary; and
- Recommendations for goal focus and priorities.

A vocational rehabilitation assessment should be completed on all patients referred to that service and should include in-depth information relative to:

- Vocational history;
- Work skills and aptitudes;
- Work skill deficits and training needs;

- Work attitudes, habits, interests, and motivations;
- Interest in and potential for training and/or practice; and
- Recommendations for programming and priority focus.

Comprehensive speech, language, and hearing evaluations are to be completed when initial screening or performance behaviors indicate that there is a deficiency or dysfunction in communication. Standardized educational assessments and an Individual Education Plan (IEP) should be completed or updated for all patients 21 years of age and younger. Such assessments and plans must meet state, federal, and local school requirements. Adult patients who are referred to education services should be assessed as appropriate; learning goals should be established in concert with treatment goals.

When a referral is made to therapeutic recreation, music, art, or movement therapy, an in-depth assessment should be completed of the area of function that relates to the problems specified in the referral. Such assessments should also include recommendations for additional treatment or for future treatment goal focus as appropriate.

It is important to emphasize that the treatment team can make appropriate referrals to rehabilitation services only when the rehabilitation staff provides them with the necessary help and information. The treatment team needs to have specific recommendations for services from the rehabilitation staff. The rehabilitation staff knows what services it can provide for which problems and needs, and this knowledge must be clearly communicated by means of specific recommendations for a given patient. The documentation of assessments, progress reports, and recommendations must be completed and available to the treatment team before treatment planning or review. The rehabilitation program coordinator is critical in facilitating such exchanges.

To facilitate the referral and progress reporting process, a referral form and a progress report form were designed for the New Jersey State System. With limited staff and centralized services, some means had to be designed for communicating a rehabilitation service referral and for documenting that the referral had been made to the appropriate rehabilitation staff. When a referral to rehabilitation services is made, the treatment team documents in the patient's clinical records that a referral has been made for a specific reason or problem and that the referral has been forwarded to the appropriate discipline. The progress report form, which is sent by the rehabilitation staff to the unit, is filed by the unit clerk in chronological order in the progress note section of the patient's clinical record. Those activity therapy and occupational therapy staff who are assigned to a unit do not use the progress report form, but rather document directly in the patient's clinical record. The referral form, however, is completed for all referrals so that services and use of resources can be monitored for the whole hospital (see Appendix).

9 PROGRAM EVALUATION AND QUALITY ASSURANCE

Lalonde (1982) states that quality assurance involves measuring the appropriateness, adequacy, and effectiveness of care given to the individual patient. A distinction is made between program evaluation and quality assurance. Program evaluation focuses on programmatic issues of accessibility, availability, cost-effectiveness, and other issues related to the program as a whole. Quality assurance, on the other hand, is oriented toward the individual client or patient. Obviously, both aspects are important and interrelated.

As part of the hospital's quality assurance and program evaluation processes, it is essential that there be a well-organized procedure for regularly reviewing each rehabilitation department's program goals and program offerings and their relevance to the rehabilitation needs of the patient population. Likewise, there should be a procedure that provides for the regular review of the rehabilitation plans of those individual patients for whom progress or response to intervention is problematic.

Rehabilitation case conferences are an excellent means of measuring the adequacy and effectiveness of intervention procedures while at the same time providing a relevant learning experience for staff. Such case conferences should be organized and run by rehabilitation staff and should be regularly scheduled in each of the divisions of the hospital (i.e., adolescent, geriatric, medical, admissions, etc.). The selection of cases for review should be based on questions or problems regarding:

- Setting treatment goals;
- Choosing appropriate intervention modalities;
- Lack of progress;
- Poor motivation;
- Management of patient behavior; and
- Aftercare or discharge planning.

The purposes of the case conference review should be to:

1. Critique the services being provided in terms of the patient's unique needs and problems;

2. Review the frequency, completeness, and relevance of rehabilitation services documentation;

3. Provide a patient-focused problem-solving forum for rehabilitation staff in which they can exchange information and share perspectives with regard to their practice and interventions with the patient; and

37

4. Make recommendations for changes in services or procedures or both to the treatment team.

The rehabilitation program coordinator in each division should be responsible, in collaboration with the staff, for the final selection of cases, for posting the conference review schedule, and for designating the meeting place. All rehabilitation staff should be encouraged to attend and to request review of specific patients about whom they have questions. Unit staff, in addition to the rehabilitation staff who are working with the patient, may be invited to attend and contribute. This is an excellent way of stimulating the interest of clinical staff in rehabilitation services and is a real impetus to improved collaboration. However, it must always be clear that this is a rehabilitation services review and that the rehabilitation staff is responsible for focus, process, and decisions. A summary of the review and recommendations should be written by the presenting member and documented by that individual in the patient's chart.

Standards for quality assurance require that the hospital and its departments have well-established, measurable goals and objectives. The integrity of an institution can be defined by the interrelationship of its overall goals with the goals and objectives of its departments. The effectiveness and adequacy of any program is measured by the extent to which its goals are met within the established time. It is essential, therefore, for rehabilitation services and each of their departments or services to have clearly established, measurable goals, with appropriate time frames, that are congruent with the goals and mission of the hospital. A format for establishing goals and objectives must be developed to include a procedure for monitoring goal attainment.

The development of goals and objectives that are measurable, and thus can provide a process for program evaluation and quality assurance, is facilitated by addressing the following questions:

1. *What* do you want to accomplish?
2. *When* do you expect to accomplish it?
3. *Who* is going to do it?
4. *How* will you know when it is completed?
5. *Who* is responsible for verifying the outcome?

For example, a goal of the education department might be to expand health education services in the transitional living unit. The objectives for achieving this goal might be to design a self-medication program, implement the self-medication program, design an alcoholism education curriculum, and implement the alcoholism program on Unit C. For each of these objectives, questions 1 through 5 would be addressed as follows:

1. *What do you want to accomplish?* Design of a self-medication program for the transitional living unit.

2. *When do you expect to accomplish it?* Curriculum design to be accomplished by March 31, 1984.

3. *Who is going to do this?* G. S. Smith, nursing instructor.

4. *How will you know when it is complete?* Course outlines will be completed and included in the education manual.

5. *Who will verify this?* J. Wilson, education department head.

An alternate format is to use a chart that is organized so that there is a column for each of the five questions for each objective. The chart system makes tracking and quarterly monitoring of progress somewhat easier than the narrative form. Sample charts in both formats are included in the Appendix.

Each department must fully review and critique the program on a yearly basis. This yearly program evaluation should include a thorough assessment of the following:

• A review of the level of functioning data for the total hospital population;

• Review of the activity interest profiles for the total patient population;

• Assessment of the relevance of the program to the cultural values and orientations of the patient population;

• Assessment of the appropriateness of the program and activities to the functional levels and interests of patients;

• Evaluation of the usefulness and appropriateness of patient assessment tools and procedures;

• Critique of schedule effectiveness and the relevance to the ward structure and schedules;

• Critique of communication process and feedback procedures with treatment team relative to patient treatment planning, implementation, and discharge planning;

• Critique of interdisciplinary collaboration within rehabilitation services and with departments outside of rehabilitation;

• Use of staff in relation to patient program needs;

• Assessment of linkages with outside resources and appropriateness, adequacy, and use;

• Critique of the comprehensiveness of services and integration among rehabilitation departments;

• Evaluation of the assessibility of services to patients;

• Assessment of the adequacy of staffing;

• Budgetary adequacy and expenditure in inventory record systems;

• Critique of supervisory patterns and effectiveness; and

• Critique of rehabilitation staff's mainstreaming in the hospital; that is, staff input and participation in hospital-wide committees and executive staff meetings.

It is essential that the ward staff be involved in the process of critiquing the program's relevance and effectiveness. This is especially important in the design of centralized hospital activity programs. A meeting with the ward staff to elicit their comments and ideas prior to any complete department critique or programmatic decisions pays considerable dividends. Likewise, a subsequent meeting with them to share the changes and recommendations that are being made will go a long way toward making a smooth transition.

One further element in program evaluation is to obtain the statistical data that make it possible to critique the use of resources, the cost-effectiveness of programs, and the breadth of services. A monthly reporting system can provide this data if the report is designed to obtain such information. Some of the questions that will provide such data are:

• How many referrals are being received monthly and from which sections of the hospital?

• To which rehabilitation services (departments) are these referrals being made?

• Are referrals and initial assessments being processed and completed in a timely manner?

• How much time is the staff spending on the assessment process?

• What does the program look like, and what are the components of the programs?

• How many patients are served by each program component?

• How much time is spent by the staff in each?

• What is the dropout rate as compared with the discharge rate?

• To what extent is the staff involved in discharge planning?

• How is staff time used? What is the proportion of time spent in direct contact with patients as compared with indirect service activities?

• What is the rate of turnover (or stability) of a patient service?

• What percentage of an appropriate patient population is being served?

The monthly report reproduced here (see Appendix) provides a structure for gathering data that are related to these questions. As it becomes possible to program such data collection into a computer, both the use and availability of information will be easier. A count of the number of different patients referred to rehabilitation services has not been uniformly possible in large state institutions. How such a figure would compare with the figure for patients with multiple referrals is a question that needs to be raised. Who are the patients who are in several programs? Who are those with only one or no referrals? These are questions that only now can begin to be addressed as rehabilitation begins to enter the computer age.

All patient work programs must conform to state and federal wage and hour regulations. When vocational rehabilitation services include contract work, transitional employment, or any other work placement programs for which a patient is paid, a record keeping and reporting system must be established in compliance with state, federal, and institutional audit and business standards. For the purpose of program evaluation and audit, a reporting format must minimally provide (in addition to data on the standard monthly report):

• The statement of monies received from each contract;

• The number of patients working, the hours worked, and wages paid;

- The balance in contract monies after wages have been paid;
- The total allocations for training or transitional employment stipends;
- The hours worked by patients and stipends paid; and
- The balance to date of stipend funds.

10 BUDGETARY PROCEDURES

Knowing what it costs to operate each service or department is a first step in budgetary planning and management. It is also necessary to know what income is generated by which services. For example, what is the reimbursement rate for physical therapy and occupational therapy services? Is a fee-for-service system a viable alternative?

Reimbursement is different for public hospitals as compared to the private sector. Most state systems are reimbursed by Medicare and Medicaid, and the states vary in terms of how costs are defined and monies allocated. Most state hospitals are reimbursed on the basis of an across the board fee that is negotiated with medical assistance. Traditionally, such an across the board fee system does not provide an incentive for developing quality rehabilitation services, because none of the disciplines is expected to produce income and the medical assistance standards for these services are general at best. In contrast, a fee-for-service reimbursement system involves establishing a fee for services that is based on an organizationally defined charge. This charge is arrived at by considering: (1) the facility's reimbursement for a given discipline's services from private, federal, or state carriers; (2) the direct and indirect costs of making the service available; and (3) the projected number of procedures (assessments, treatments, etc.) for the established budget period. A good resource for developing such a formula is the material presented by Baum (1983). Under this system there is financial incentive to provide reimbursible services and thus to meet the standards for services set by the carriers.

Reimbursement income significantly influences budget decisions. It is extremely important to know the reimbursement contract, to know which rehabilitation services are and are not covered, and then to negotiate for coverage.

In estimating costs, the most tangible figures are staff salaries. For planning purposes, the recommended staffing ratios for each of the disciplines should be used. Estimating and/or budgeting for operational funds is another matter, and it is this formula that has remained elusive in the rehabilitation services. The traditional way of handling this has been to use the previous year's costs plus a cost of living percentage. This procedure, however, does not accommodate or encourage changes in services or programs.

One simple way to begin to get a perspective on costs is to add up the amount of money spent for supplies and equipment by a given department for the year. Then divide this figure by the average number of patients serviced by that department during the year. This provides a figure that reflects an average cost of materials per patient per year, exclusive of facility maintenance and salaries. If necessary, this figure can then be adjusted upward or downward according to what is perceived as minimal for quality service.

When a cost per patient can be ascertained, it becomes possible to estimate an increase or decrease in costs on the basis of case load. For example, in a given hospital, for each occupational therapy staff person who is hired, the cost will be the salary plus $750 per year for supplies and equipment for a case load of 25 patients. To compute the total cost of a department, salaries are added to supplies and equipment costs as well as utilities, maintenance, and other indirect costs. Such estimates, when kept over a period of time, should provide the data necessary to arrive at a formula that is more estimate than "guess-timate."

It is essential for rehabilitation services to be involved in the process of estimating costs for operating each department, in budget preparation, and in the decision-making process regarding allocations. This involves having each department generate a budget request based on their clearly articulated goals and objectives with justifications and time frames for implementation. Once allocations to each department have been made, each must be responsible for monitoring expenditures.

11 PROGRAM PLANNING AND STRATEGIES FOR CHANGE

Too often the issue that is addressed first in planning the development or redirection of a program is what changes must be made rather than what the service model should look like. Planning for change must be preceded by the gathering of data; a program design should be developed on the basis of those data. The changes that will need to be made are defined in terms of what the projected program plan looks like and how this differs from current structure and operation. Thus, the questions always are: Where are we now? And where, on the basis of the plan, do we need to be tomorrow and the day after?

To design a plan and bring about the necessary changes in a system, you must first know what kind of information you need to have about the system. Below are some of the areas of information that are needed before any decision with regard to program plan or change can be made.

• *Purpose of the Institution/Agency.* What are the objectives of the institution in providing service? Is the institution part of a larger system? What is the purpose of this system and what is its mission?

• *Program/Service Orientation.* What is the philosophy that governs the institution's management of health problems and its delivery system? What forces influence and shape the delivery system?

• *Client/Patient Population.* What is the age span and social, cultural, and educational profile of the patient population? What are the characteristics of admissions? What are the major diagnostic categories? The length of stay? The level of functioning of the patients? What is the nature of the environment (e.g., urban, rural, industrial, agricultural) that the hospital serves?

• *Services.* What professional services are provided and what is the ratio of professional to paraprofessional in each department? What is the staff-patient ratio in each department? How do each of the sevices define their primary area of responsibility for patient care? What services and programs are provided by each profession with what percentage of the patient population? What is the treatment philosophy of the institution? Where do rehabilitation concepts fit within this philosophy? What is the supervisory pattern for the professional departments? To whom are they accountable? What seems to be the status of each department? How do they view one another? What seems to be the level and kind of power and influence of the clinical director? To whom are the rehabilitation services (departments) responsible? What seems to be the status and crediblity of each rehabilitation service department?

• *Organizational-Administrative Structure.* What are the lines of authority? Who is responsible to whom? How are administrative decisions really made? How are clinical and programmatic decisions made? What are the communication patterns? Who talks to whom? What are the critical decision-making committees and subcommittees? Who belongs to them? How are decisions made relative to allocation of resources (space and staffing), budget, and patient treatment? Where do monies come from? How is money allocated? What does the last Medicare survey report say? What does the JCAH survey report say?

Such information is gathered from institutional and agency reports, from interviews and discussion with the chief administrator, clinical director, and other key staff, and from observations and listening with the "third ear." Once a perspective is obtained, then work can begin on developing a service plan. On the basis of the data gathered, what are the characteristic strengths and assets of the institution? What are the characteristic problems and deficiencies? Which service needs are being only partially met? Which service needs are not being responded to? Which rehabilitation services should be provided for which populations? What should be the focus and components of each of these services? How should these services be interrelated with other rehabilitation services and with clinical services? What resources (staffing, space, equipment, and finances) will be needed for each?

Given the information about the institution, what should be the priorities? What should be the schedule for phase-in? What time frames are reasonable? With whom will you need to communicate for phase-in? For what purposes?

There is no recipe for success or for a fail-safe format for bringing about change. However, there are a few basic principles that seem to reduce the chanciness of interventions. Many of these are well known but need to be restated periodically.

It is critical that you and the person to whom you will be accountable have a clear agreement about the nature and purpose of the job for which you are contracting. This includes clarifying (1) the expectations of both in terms of outcomes (i.e., what it is you are expected to do and what *you* would like or expect to do) and (2) specifically what authority you have in carrying out your responsibilites (i.e., who is accountable to you and which programmatic decisions are yours to make). Such an understanding is crucial, especially if systems change is an expectation, because you will need to have one another's support and understanding if your goals are to be realized. The management level of the person to whom you are accountable will define the influence and power that you may exercise.

Working through such an agreement and taking on the responsibility of a change agent requires that you know what you are about. This means knowing your profession, having a clear idea of what it is and what it is not, and knowing and being comfortable with your expertise as well as areas where your knowledge or skill are limited. It means having enough information about the system to be clear about what you perceive as its needs. It means knowing and being clear about what you can offer and what expertise you bring that will address the system's problem and needs.

Once into the system, you will need to establish alliances with those who formally and informally make or influence the important decisions. Each department head and section chief has expectations, pet projects, and problems. Listen and identify which of these problems, interests, and concerns can be responded to by your programmatic interventions. If the interests and concerns of others can be incorporated into your plans, then work collaboratively on the change. Success is more likely when the change that is proposed is responsive to a key person's problems or concerns.

Planned change—in fact, any deviation from a customary way of doing things—is frequently threatening. The "new way" alters the predictability of people's situations and is thus chancy and risky. Fear of and resistance to the new and unknown can be reduced to the extent that the individuals can be helped to feel that they have some control over what is happening. Thus, it is critical to involve the staff in some of the planning for implementation and in the problem solving that they will be expected to implement. The importance of your relationship with the staff who will be expected to implement change cannot be overemphasized. It is essential to be clear about your expectations and your values, what you expect from them, and what you can offer them. Hear their problems and concerns and ask them for their ideas and perspectives. The more they are actively involved in describing the changes needed, solving problems, and setting priorities and time frames, the less resistance there will be. However, it must always be clear that the final decision rests with you. There is a need always to work on clarifying and defining: (1) What decisions are you personally responsible for? (2) What decisions must be made with others? and (3) What decisions belong elsewhere and are out of your realm?

Begin with those changes that are most likely to succeed, have the least risk, and where the need is acknowledged by most staff. Such action ensures an early success and establishes your credibility. The first move should be as risk-free as possible. The more difficult and complex changes should be addressed as your credibility and the staff's trust in you builds and as you develop alliances and support systems.

Resist the temptation to influence and change people by talking or lecturing to them. Instead demonstrate it—do it! For example, in one hospital there were all sorts of misconceptions about occupational therapy and little regard for a rehabilitation perspective. Instead of developing orientation materials and an inservice program, it was decided to immediately implement an activity program on the ward with the most administrative problems. The program was designed, the paraprofessional activity staff was rapidly trained, and the program was implemented.

The impact on patients and staff was so marked that no talk about the value of occupational therapy was necessary. The change in ward milieu and patient behavior was the talk of the hospital, and the demand for occupational therapy from staff in other areas of the hospital was impressive. This demonstration was worth more than a thousand words or hours of inservice programs. However, one other factor was critical—the choice of the demonstration project. It was, in essence, fail-safe. Any intervention that have provided a structured daily program of activities consistent with the level of functioning of the patients was bound to reduce nursing and ward management problems by reducing less regressive behaviors of the patients. The most inexperienced occupational therapist knows this and would have been able to predict success. There was no resistance from nursing staff, because they were deliberately not asked or expected to participate. Their level of frustration and fatigue was high, and they were relieved that someone was going to help them. Asking them to help at the start would have added to their burden. Once the program was successful, they willingly participated.

It is important to get to know the hospital, the wards, and the three shifts of staff as well as the patients. Time should be spent with staff who work on evenings and weekends as well as visiting programs and wards during the day. Change is difficult and the process involves long hours. The change process is not a 9-to-5 job.

With each program that is developed, build into it a system or process for evaluating outcomes. It is critical to be able to document changes in patient behavior and function. Programs are designed to help patients; therefore, the success and credibility of what is being done must be measured by changes that occur in patient performance. The ward activity mentioned earlier had a built-in patient assessment formula. It is a simple matter to rate the patient population before a program has begun and then at regular intervals throughout the program to measure impact and the extent to which the established goals are being met.

Bring in with you—or have the capability of hiring soon after you arrive—a person who shares your perspective and philosophy, one who comfortably understands risk and with whom you collaborate and work. This provides the collaborative support you will need, and the person's arrival reinforces the goal of change in the system. The addition of this person to the staff will strengthen the commitment to change. When vacancies occur or new positions are created, the selection of staff is a critical matter. Try to recruit people who are bright and energetic, with a hard core of pragmatism and an excitement about learning how to turn a system around.

The force field analysis developed by Kurt Lewin is a useful model for planning for change and reducing the chanciness or unpredictability of outcomes. In discussing the application of this model, Benne and Birnbaum (1960) describe several principles of strategy for effecting change. They are:

1. *To change a subsystem or any part of a subsystem, relevant aspects of the environment must also be changed.* For example, to institute a prevocational patient group on the ward in the morning (when patients are more alert) will require changing the time of community meetings and dealing with all of the forces that are supporting the status quo. Unless this is worked out, there will be conflict—and probably no patients for the prevocational group.

2. *To change behavior on any one level of a hierarchical organization, it is necessary to achieve complementary and reinforcing changes in organizational levels above and below that level.* A decision was made to change the responsibilities for patient escort to occupational and activity therapy programs because it was evident that an extensive amount of professional time was being spent in escorting patients, an activity that would be more cost-effectively done by ward aides or ward technicians. This change altered the duties and responsibilities of the charge nurse, the program coordinator, the professional occupational therapy staff, the occupational therapy assistants, and the ward aides. Without considering and working out all the lines of responsibility and authority and alterations in responsibilities, the change will not be implemented. The restraining forces are simply too strong.

3. *The place to begin change is at those points in the system where stress and strain exists. Stress may give rise to dissatisfaction with the status quo and thus become a motivating factor for change in the system.* The example of the ward activity program mentioned earlier is a good illustration of this principle. There was little or no resistance to changing the entire schedule and the roles of the nursing staff on the ward because dissatisfaction was so high.

4. *In diagnosing the possibility of change in an institution, it is always necessary to assess the degree of stress and strain at points where change is sought. One should ordinarily avoid beginning change at the point of greatest stress.* As an example, look again at the first principle and the issue of a prevocational group replacing a community meeting on the schedule. In one environment, the status of the community meeting was so high that resistance to changing the time would have been fierce. To begin a program of change by attempting such a schedule change in this division would have resulted in a struggle and failure. On another division, the community meeting was not particularly valued by staff, and the change in schedule was not a problem. Only some time later was it reasonable to approach the first division to work out changes for patient services that touched on ward schedules.

5. *If thoroughgoing changes in a heirachical structure are desirable or necessary, change should ordinarily start with the policy-making body.* Self-medication programs have been viewed as a critical component of the predischarge program of the hospital. In those instances where the medical director and the chief executive officer support the idea that patients should assume

responsibility for their own medication, the programs have worked well. In those institutions where the medical director or the chief executive feels unsure and is concerned about risk, the programs are weak and problems have existed. In the same manner, when those at the top of the hierarchy strongly and openly support rehabilitation services, the rehabilitation programs are strong and successful. When support for these program services is tentative, the programs are weak and poorly attended.

6. *Both the formal and informal organization of an institution must be considered in planning any process of change.*   Every system has a network of informal groups or "clubs" that influence and sometimes control decisions and any attempts at change. Knowing about these informal groups and understanding their specific leverage and power is essential. Frequently the strategy of choice is to develop an alliance with the leader or an influential member of the group and then to work to obtain their support in an effort that pays some dividends to them.

7. *The effectiveness of a planned change is often directly related to the degree to which members at all levels of an institutional hierarchy take part in the fact-finding and the diagnosing of needed changes and in the formulating and reality-testing of goals and programs of change.*   The degree to which those who will be affected by change are active participants in the change process is the degree to which the desire to maintain the status quo will be dissipated. For example, in one institution where resistance to the new director (who had been hired to change the system) was very high, the supervisors from all of the departments were brought together as the change-coordinating committee. This opportunity to influence the nature and timing of changes that they would have to implement helped significantly to reduce their resistance. Over a period of time, most members of that coordinating group became involved in and actively committed to some aspect of the change process. Although the department heads never vigorously campaigned for the change, after several months they no longer actively resisted it, and the plans for change were able to proceed.

Finally, use your intuition, then test it out with data. Being a change agent means making it possible for others to construct and experience a better place.

12 TASK AND ACTIVITY GROUP PROTOCOLS

The following material consists of selected protocols for a variety of task, activity, and work groups. These protocols were developed by the activity therapy and occupational therapy staff at Springfield Hospital Center, Maryland, and at Greystone Park Psychiatric Hospital, New Jersey. They are reproduced here to provide examples of different protocol styles, to reflect the diversity of task or activity group focuses, and to provide a perspective on the kinds of programming provided for the long-term chronic schizophrenic hospital patient.

LEISURE PLANNING

Purpose
To facilitate exploration and awareness of leisure interests, skills, talents, and abilities; to facilitate the development of leisure skills; to provide opportunities for structured planning and cooperative decision making concerning group leisure experiences; to assist the patient in overcoming barriers to participation; to offer "fun" leisure experiences as a laboratory for learning and practicing leisure skills; to educate the patient about leisure opportunities in the community and to provide exposure to community resources.

Rationale
Individual activity patterns are often lost with the onset of mental illness. Since these activity patterns are the expression of the individual's proper use and appreciation of time, the loss of these patterns results in reality disorientation. The patient loses contact with others, with environment, and with time.

Specific deficits noted in the occupational therapy screening assessment of the population included an apparent lack of involvement in purposeful leisure-time pursuits and an inability to identify satisfying leisure-time interests. Several possible factors may be contributing to these deficits:

• limited self-awareness concerning one's strengths, skills, present and past accomplishments, personal goals, beliefs, and values;
• lack of adequate planning skills;
• pragmatic barriers to participation, such as a locked ward, finances, lack of transportation, lack of equipment, lack of skills, or lack of opportunity;

- limited knowledge of resources and how to use them; or
- lack of underlying competencies in sensorimotor skills, cognitive skills, interpersonal skills needed to participate and experience pleasure.

In addition, the activities histories of this patient population generally reveal a sparse repertoire of childhood play experiences on which to base adult leisure experiences. Play has been widely recognized as the child's arena for learning and practicing the rules and social skills necessary for subsequent life roles in school, work, and recreation. Play or leisure competencies need to be developed along with other activities of daily living and may, in fact, facilitate the development of other functional roles (such as work).

A basic premise of occupational therapy is that time is best structured by the performance of activity. One primary focus of this program is the weekly activity trip in the community. The purpose of the community trip is to have fun and to offer opportunities to learn or practice basic leisure skills. Mutually shared fun experiences are more conducive to involvement and participation than verbal leisure counseling techniques. However, isolated community trips are not enough to develop the self-awareness, knowledge, and skills needed to independently plan and execute leisure activities after discharge. The patients will take an active role in the planning and implementation of leisure activities to improve their planning skills as well as to broaden awareness of self and community resources. In addition, an active role in planning will increase patients' motivation to participate. The planning process will be accomplished through consensual decision making to foster group identity.

Patient Selection Criteria
- Poor use of free time;
- Poor leisure planning skills;
- Inability to identify leisure interests;
- Ability to attend to task or discussion for at least a 15-minute time span; and
- Adequate degree of socially acceptable behavior to warrant community exposure.

Goals
- Improved use of free time;
- Improved ability to plan for leisure time;
- Clarification of leisure values;
- Recognition of leisure interests and options;
- Acquisition of knowledge concerning community resources and use of resources; and
- Experience pleasure in a group leisure experience.

Group Structure
Two distinct group sessions are planned each week as part of this program.

1. *Exploration and Planning Session* to meet once a week for 1 hour. Enabling activities will be provided to identify interests and clarify values (i.e., collages or scrapbooks of activities). The group will plan a variety of group leisure experiences. Practical constraints such as time, money, and transportation will be discussed and resolved. Communication media (e.g., newspapers) will be used to identify leisure options and community resources. Group members will also be helped to keep a weekly activity schedule and encouraged to established concrete goals for individual leisure pursuits. The role of the group leader will be to provide support and structure and to set limits as necessary.

2. *Activity and Evaluation Session* to meet once a week for 2 hours. The patients will carry out the group community trip planned in the previous session. The community trips will provide exposure to community resources through a variety of leisure experiences in physical, cultural, educational, and social activities. The role of the leader will be primarily as a participant and role model. After each community trip, the leader will be responsible for structuring a brief feedback session, using a satisfaction questionnaire to evaluate members' responses to each activity experience.

Program Discharge Criteria
- Discharge from the hospital;
- Excessive absences;
- Involvement in a vocational program in the community during normal working hours; or
- Independent pursuit of one or more leisure interests in the community.

Reevaluation/Monitoring Procedures
- Periodic time mosaics and activity configurations; and
- Observations and progress notes with respect to stated goals.

YOUNG ADULTS GROUP

Purpose
To provide opportunities for cooperative, goal-directed experiences in a relatively unstressful social environment; to stimulate and support communication; to facilitate the development and maintenance of peer relationships; to provide clarity and consistency in relationships with authority figures; to offer leisure opportunities relevant to developmental needs and prospective community placements; to offer healthy, fun experiences that also require ongoing interpersonal and situational coping skills; to present opportunities for the group's service to others through a variety of cooperative tasks and projects.

Rationale

One of the outstanding issues for young adults is the need to feel productive and autonomous. There are, however, fundamental deficits among this group of residents that often interfere with gainful employment and independence. These deficits relate, in part, to the interpersonal and situational coping skills required to engage in work settings in peer and/or subordinate roles.

Such skills begin to develop in childhood play when group norms, rules for play, and social relationships emerge. These are critical developmental milestones related to the individual's entry into future life roles. The occupational therapy assessments completed with this patient population indicate a lack of social skills and a paucity of relationships with contemporaries. Fundamental social skills and comfort with peers are prerequisites for entering an interpersonally stress-laden world of work. Consequently, this program's initial focus will address the need to relate to one's contemporaries. The modality used to provide such learning experiences will include a variety of leisure-time activities appropriate to the developmental needs and cultural orientations of the patient group.

Leisure activities require varying kinds and degrees of skill competency. Development of a given skill is impetus for engaging and relating to others. The sense of pleasure and fun inherent in leisure activities makes dialogue and communication a more comfortable, natural process. In addition, purposeful participation in such activities begins to address the issues of autonomy and productivity. As a cohesive group develops, other experiences will be provided that call for cooperative group efforts focused on providing a service or product for others, thus further facilitating a sense of individual efficacy and peer group identity. The significance of being able to identify with a valued, productive group cannot be overstated, particularly considering these patients' psychosocial and psychosexual developmental levels.

Patient Selection Criteria

- 18–30-year-old age range;
- Ability to tolerate and attend to group experiences for at least 20-minute periods;
- Demonstrated difficulty identifying and pursuing realistic and personally satisfying leisure activities;
- Demonstrated difficulty entering peer relationships or maintaining peer coping skills; and
- Demonstrated difficulty experiencing pleasure in planned or spontaneous events.

Goals

- Improved ability to make decisions and solve problems;
- Enhanced perception of self as being able to influence events;

- Consistent identification of alternative behavioral responses for a variety of pertinent life situations and issues;
- Increased repertoire of interpersonal skills necessary to function in cooperative group enterprises;
  - Increased awareness of others' feelings;
  - Engagement in and maintenance of social relationships with peers; and
  - Active, meaningful use of leisure time.

Group Structure
- The group shall consist of no more than 20 residents, meeting two evenings and one afternoon per week;
- Initial emphasis on leisure experiences, varied in their requirements for participation (i.e., cognitive, perceptual-motor, psychosocial), reflecting individuals' functional capacities;
- Exploration of group and individual experiences and their prospective relevance to other situations;
- Use of those activities that intrinsically facilitate verbal and nonverbal communication;
- Use of activities that employ and demonstrate the varying degrees of role delineation in relation to authority figures;
- Eventual provision of activities designed to offer a "doing for others" experience; and
- A structure that will eventually allow and support spontaneous group activities and activities selected and planned by group members.

Program Discharge Criteria
- Discharge from hospital;
- Involvement in community leisure or service groups;
- Persistent absenteeism (as determined by occupational therapist);
- Continuing inability to function within group and follow group protocols; or
- Criteria that may emerge from group members concerning continued group membership requirements.

Reevaluation/Monitoring Procedures
- Observation of patients' participation and interactions;
- Patients' subjective statements; and
- Development of Appropriate Peer and Adult Interaction Skill Rating Scale.

WORK SKILLS DEVELOPMENT I

Purpose
To provide work-oriented experiences in a supportive, structured group setting as an intermediate step toward involvement in community programs; to present graded work experiences designed to improve task behaviors (i.e., concentration, attention span, time management, frustration tolerance, perceptual-motor skills); to offer opportunities for the development of individual role identities and a group identity; to facilitate the development of interpersonal coping skills relevant to being a work group member; to promote group leisure planning; to provide reality-based budgeting and money management activities that correspond to individuals' productivity in a work group.

Rationale
There is wide spectrum of work-related skills that also contribute to other areas of life. The human work experience is not restricted to a particular task at hand, but is connected to those around us and to our environment outside the work setting. The required components of this experience (cognitive, psychosocial, perceptual-motor) are pragmatically related to handling personal finances in order to meet basic needs and engage in pleasurable leisure activities alone and with others. This pragmatic relationship is not discrete; rather, it is a global association.

Currently, there are a substantial number of residents in need of supportive and structured work-related experiences. These individuals exhibit poor task behaviors (frustration tolerance, cognitive skills, perceptual-motor performance) as well as limited interpersonal skills and avocational involvements. The complexity and fundamental nature of this array of deficits limits the benefits available in community vocational programs. Consequently, the need for comprehensive, practical programming in this direction with community-oriented objectives is clear.

Patient Selection Criteria
   • Ability to tolerate and attend to a task or group focus for at least 20-minute periods;
   • Demonstrated inability to consistently engage in work or work-related experiences;
   • Demonstrated difficulty or limited experience in handling personal finances; and
   • Previous unsuccessful or terminated sheltered work experiences.

Goals
   • Improved task behaviors relevant to particular goal-directed experiences;
   • Increased repertoire of interpersonal skills necessary to function in

cooperative group enterprises with peers and authority figures;

- Development of money management skills applicable to meeting basic needs and engaging in avocational experiences;
- Improved ability to engage in and handle ongoing vocational experiences;
- Development of individuals' sense of belonging to an interdependent and productive work community; and
- Improved sense of individuals' productivity and ability to effect change on external environment.

Group Structure
- The group shall consist of a maximum of 10 residents who have been referred jointly to occupational therapy and vocational rehabilitation.
- Occupational therapy sessions are held twice weekly for 1 hour.
- Work tasks provided during occupational therapy sessions require collaborative efforts by group members, thus facilitating interdependent work roles and peer communication.
- Money earned during occupational therapy sessions is placed in a group fund, overseen by the occupational therapist, to be used for a group activity decided on by the members.
- Occupational therapy sessions include the group's calculation of money earned and the amount of money required for various group activities and group planning to determine which group activities are feasible.
- Opportunities for peer review and expression of work attitudes and goals are incorporated into occupational therapy sessions' protocol.
- Group members have individual work schedules during their vocational rehabilitation sessions (2 days/week).
- Individuals' work assignments in vocational rehabilitation require their parallel participation with supervision from vocational rehabilitation staff.
- Money earned during vocational rehabilitation sessions is spent or saved according to each individual's discretion.

Program Discharge Criteria
- Discharge from hospital;
- Involvement in community vocational training;
- Persistent absenteeism (as determined by occupational therapist);
- Continuing inability to function within the group and follow group protocols; and
- Attainment of designated treatment goals, indicating readiness for less structured vocational experiences.

Reevaluation/Monitoring Procedures
- Observation of patients' participation and interaction;
- Patients' subjective statements;
- Etheridge Pre-Vocational Evaluation of Rehabilitation Potential.

WORK SKILLS GROUP

Purpose
To provide a structured work experience within a small group setting; to develop basic task skills and preliminary functional work habits (engagement, dependability, punctuality, concentration, problem solving); to develop the social behaviors needed in a work setting; and to determine readiness for referral to the vocational rehabilitation department.

Rationale
A review of the patient population reveals a number of patients who have had chronic difficulty in work situations both within the hospital and in the community. They resist attending programs because of negative past experiences, which are directly related to task skill and interpersonal deficits. Many are threatened by large group settings, and some refuse task groups, viewing them as juvenile. The development of a small work group in a non-threatening atmosphere with individual supervision to guide and ensure success and satisfaction seems appropriate. The acquisition of task and social skills in this setting will allow for greater success in the more formal work setting in the vocational rehabilitation department as well as in work situations outside of the hospital.

Patient Selection Criteria
- Lack of successful or rewarding work experiences;
- Willing to attend group on a regular basis;
- Lack of involvement in other vocational programs;
- Able to tolerate a small group setting; and
- Deficits in the task and/or social skills needed to sustain employment.

Specific Treatment Objectives
- Improve consistency of skills needed for task completion (concentration, problem solving, engagement);
- Improve ability to engage in and sustain ongoing task;
- Improve social-interpersonal skills (cooperation, sociability, responsibility);
- Develop self-concept as a worker; and
- Ongoing evaluation to determine readiness for vocational rehabilitation.

Group Structure
- Group will meet four times a week for a total of 4 hours.
- Group Size: optimum 6.
- Group Structure: Parallel/project task group with each person's earnings based on individual productivity.
- Media: The major media will be prevocational piece work tasks.

- Tasks will be determined by the leader, who serves as a role model and facilitator.
- Immediate reinforcements may be used in the form of candy and gum with long-term reinforcement through bi-weekly paychecks.

Program Discharge Criteria
- Discharge from hospital or transfer to another unit within the hospital;
- Involvement in hospital or community-based vocational rehabilitation program; and
- Excessive absences.

Reevaluation/Monitoring Procedures
- Objective measures of productivity and consistency of attendance through time sheets and earnings;
- Observations of patient population, performance, and interactions;
- Patients' subjective comments; and
- Documentation of progress toward stated group objectives and individual goals.

PREVOCATIONAL TRAINING

Purpose
To provide a structured, time-limited work experience within a small group setting as a step toward full-time vocational involvement, either within the hospital setting or in the community; to develop basic task skills and preliminary work habits (engagement, concentration, neatness, problem solving, responsibility, punctuality) through the use of assembly line packaging tasks and social interaction with other group members; to provide an opportunity for budgeting and management of group monies earned through completion of projects.

Rationale
There are a number of residents who are not actively engaged in any vocational program or preparation. Historically, these individuals exhibit difficulty sustaining part-time or full-time sheltered or competitive employment. They are resistant to attending programs because of negative past experiences, which are directly related to task-skill and interpersonal deficits. A shared group experience using simple assembly-line activities will encourage engagement and teach those basic group skills that are necessary for (1) effective individual and group relationships and (2) engagement in other work experiences within the hospital and the community.

Patient Selection Criteria
- Lack of involvement in a vocational program;

- Previous difficulty sustaining sheltered work experiences; and
- Ability to concentrate for periods of at least 30 minutes.

Specific Treatment Objectives
- Improve consistency of skills needed for task completion (engagement, concentration, problem solving);
- Improve ability to engage in and sustain ongoing vocational experiences (punctuality, responsibility);
- Improve social-interpersonal skills (cooperation, sociability, responsibility);
- Develop basic money management skills (budgeting and buying); and
- Improve perception of self as an effective, influential being.

Group Structure
- Time and length of meetings: group meets 3 times weekly for a total of 3 hours.
- Size of group: optimum 8.
- Group methods and procedures:
    1. Leader initially determines task selection, breaks down task, and allocates duties.
    2. Leader serves as a role model and facilitator, engaging all members and eliciting appropriate responses.
    3. Leader will allow for increasing responsibility and independence of group members with respect to spending money.

Program Discharge Criteria
- Readiness for hospital or community-based vocational training programs;
- Excessive absences; and
- Discharge from hospital.

Reevaluation/Monitoring Procedures
- Observations of patients' participation, performance, and interactions;
- Patients' subjective comments; and
- Documentation of progress toward stated group objectives and individual goals.

WORK SKILLS DEVELOPMENT II

Purpose
To improve task and social behaviors to a state of readiness for participation in the programs offered by the vocational rehabilitation department.

Rationale
Essential to the success of work adjustment training programs is the development of a recognized developmental hierarchy of attitudes and concepts. The elements of this hierarchy include: handling of frustration; willingness to accept help; responsibility; dependability; independence; and internalized understanding of what a job is, why people work, and the importance of personal relationships. Task occupation is an integral part of normal living, and activity is the agent through which human beings learn and develop. Actual work tasks will be used to develop basic work attitudes and readiness for more formalized vocational rehabilitation.

Patient Selection Criteria
The rehabilitation services initial assessment will be used to determine education background, work experience, work history, and interests. This will be supplemented by other available assessment data.

Specific Referral Criteria
- Poor work or work adjustment history or sparse work history;
- Interest in participation in the work skills group with eventual participation in the vocational rehabilitation prevocational program;
- Poor frustration tolerance;
- Distractibility with inability to attend to a given task for 1 hour;
- Poor task skills; and
- Deficit in social interpersonal skills that effect work adjustment behavior.

Specific Treatment Objectives
- Develop self-concept as a worker;
- Improve concentration;
- Reduce stress associated with vocational rehabilitation through skill mastery and familiarity with work tasks (increase ego strength and ability to tolerate stress);
- Improve ability to perceive cause-and-effect relationships through development of time and money concepts;
- Ongoing evaluation to determine readiness for vocational rehabilitation;
- Normalize work-related behaviors; and
- Improve motivation or work readiness.

61

Group Structure
- The major media of the group will be prevocational piece work tasks.
- Group structure: Parallel/project task group with each person's earnings based on individual productivity.
- Task and environment will be modified to maximize the opportunity for success (e.g., distraction-free environment, refocusing by the therapist, task analysis, positive reinforcers);
- Each session will run for up to 1 hour with immediate reinforcement (e.g., gum, candy) and long-term reinforcement through bi-weekly paychecks;
- A variety of techniques will be used to aid in the development of time and money concepts and self-concept as a worker; and
- Prior to discharge from the work skills group and referral to the vocational rehabilitation department, the patient will visit the vocational rehabilitation area and be introduced to the staff to aid smooth transition into the vocational rehabilitation program.

Reevaluation/Monitoring Procedures
- Objective measure of productivity, and consistency of attendance through bi-weekly time sheets;
- Weekly assessment of work-related behaviors: need for refocusing, close supervision, problem-solving ability, quality of work, frustration tolerance (response to external control), adherence to rules, goal-setting ability; and
- Consistency of task performance and behavior.

Program Discharge Criteria
- Patient meets requirements for involvement in the vocational rehabilitation program as outlined in the rehabilitation services department referral criteria guide (i.e., concentration on a task for a minimum of 1 hour without a break);
- Transfer from acute care or admissions unit or discharged from the hospital; and
- Consistent refusal to attend work skills group.

TASK GROUP

Purpose
To develop basic task skills, body awareness, and a sense of self as well as preliminary functional work habits through interaction with suitable nonhuman objects and activities selected to develop these skills.

Rationale
An individual cannot survive in the community if he or she is unable to perform simple activities and interact with other people. Thus, the patient must acquire both task skills and group interaction skills. These skills are fundamental to many of the things one must do to satisfy needs and contribute to the community.

In the normal course of development, many task skills are learned through play. This is an ideal situation for learning such skills: failure is unimportant, pressure is minimal, and the chance for experimentation is high. Unfortunately, many people reach adulthood without acquiring these skills. Due to high self and societal expectations for successful performance, it is more difficult to attain task skills as an adult.

Creating an unstressful group situation that allows for short-term successes and mastery over tools and the environment provides an ideal situation for the development of much needed task skills and a firmer sense of self.

Patient Selection Criteria
- Availability for treatment;
- Willing to attend group;
- Ability to tolerate group setting; and
- Identified by occupational therapy assessment as having moderate to maximum difficulty with task skills such as: initial and prolonged engagement, attention span/concentration, following a sequence of verbal directions, attending to detail, manipulating tools and supplies, and pacing speed during given time period.

Specific Treatment Objectives
- Improve consistency of skills needed for task completion;
- Increase awareness of self;
- Enhance perception of self as being able to influence environment and events; and
- Increase productive behaviors that lead to the identification and fulfillment of individual needs.

Group Structure
- Time and length of meeting: group meets twice a week for a total of 2 hours.
- Size of Group: optimum 10, maximum 12, minimum 8.

- Group Methods and Procedures

1. Task modality will be introduced in a sequential, developmental order: fingerpainting, clay, papier-mâché, leather.

2. The structure within each modality will be graded as follows:

 a. Each will progress from maximum to minimum structure, using creative processes from concrete to abstract.

 b. Staff's role and intervention will decrease.

 c. Tasks will progress from individual to group endeavors.

3. The long-term structure of the group, spanning all modalities, will be graded as follows:

 a. Staff's role will decrease.

 b. The amount of initial structure given will decrease with each consecutive modality.

 c. Time spent on each modality will increase as attention span and ability to sustain engagement increases.

Program Discharge Criteria

- Discharge from hospital;
- Excessive absences;
- Involvement in vocational program in the community during normal working hours; and
- Resolution of task skill deficiencies noted on admission to group.

Reevaluation/Monitoring Procedures

- Observations of individual and group progress.
- An ongoing individualized performance evaluation will be updated after each group meeting, noting progress and deficiencies in areas of concern.
- Verbal processing of group and individual maturation.

TASK SKILLS—WORK GROUP

Purpose

To focus on developing specific skills and behaviors related to work adjustment, including time management, task organization, dependability, work tolerance, basic elements of work skills (stapling, taping, filing, hand tools, etc.), vocational exploration, ability to take constructive criticism and accept worker role, improved work-related productivity, and reality testing in a work setting.

Rationale

In Western culture, "work" is given a great deal of emphasis. Financial payment, personal satisfaction, and accomplishment are all derived from work.

Unfortunately, many people with psychiatric problems have never developed work skills or have lost them after hospitalization; therefore, work is used as a modality because of its normalizing and reinforcing effects.

Patient Selection Criteria
- Lack of recent work experience;
- Level of function at level 3 for all or most categories;
- Values worker role;
- Demonstrated difficulties in sequencing, time management, work tolerance, and sustaining interest; and
- Ability to concentrate on an organized task for a period of at least 20 minutes.

Goals
Development of the following specific skills and behaviors related to work adjustment to the level that will meet criteria for entry into compensated workshop or on-the-job training program.
- Learning basic work skills, such as stapling, taping, assembly, etc.;
- Developing dependability;
- Managing time;
- Improving work tolerance;
- Organizing and sequencing task;
- Learning to take criticism; and
- Improving productivity.

Group Structure
- Group will meet 4 times a week for 1-hour sessions.
- Work projects will be geared to functional level of the patient with the complexity and time involved in the program increased in accordance with progress. The ultimate goal is to be able to sustain a 2-hour block of time in the main vocational rehabilitation building/workshop.

Discharge Criteria
- Discharge from hospital;
- Referral to vocational rehabilitation program;
- Excessive absences;
- Inability to cope with tasks; and
- Continual disruptive behaviors.

HOME ARTS PROGRAM

Description
The home arts program is designed to provide patients with an informal "home" atmosphere for developing and enhancing homemaking skills. The focus is on activities of daily living (i.e., grooming, laundry, personal shopping, budgeting, special diets), social skills, didactic and group skills, and leisure activities.

Goals
- Increase sense of competence in home management skills;
- Improve ability to plan, organize, and carry out daily living tasks; and
- Develop ability to share, make decisions, trust self and others, elicit positive responses from others, and learn basic self-reliance skills.

Referral Criteria
- Possibility of discharge to group home or apartment;
- Social isolation, difficulty initiating contact and engaging with others; and
- Lack of basic homemaking skills or experience.

Course Outline
1. Meal preparation
   a. Meal preparation
   b. Menu planning
   c. Table setting
   d. Meal clean-up
   e. Preparing shopping list
   f. Operating large and small appliances
   g. Appropriate use of kitchen equipment and utensils
2. Nutrition
   a. Knowledge of Basic 4
   b. Calorie values
   c. Special diets (where applicable)
3. Housekeeping
   a. Dust
   b. Vacuum/sweep
   c. House cleaning
   d. Household product information
4. Self-care skills
   a. Appearance
   b. Appropriate dress
   c. Posture
   d. Personal hygiene (including hair and nail care)
   e. Make-up (if applicable)

    f. Laundry

    g. Personal shopping

    h. Basic first aid

    i. Safety precautions

    j. Emergency procedure

5. Play/leisure skills

    a. Exercise for toning and relaxation

    b. Exploration of leisure activities: crafts, reading, small group games, music, and dance

6. Sewing

    a. Mending and repairing clothing

    b. Sewing on buttons

    c. Hemming

7. Social skills

    a. Communicating with others, conversational skills

    b. Telephone use

    c. Table etiquette

    d. Current events (newspapers)

8. Community trips

    a. Grocery store

    b. Shopping malls

    c. Restaurant

    d. Private invitations

Discharge Criteria

- Achieved goals: demonstrated readiness to enter transitional program;
- Discharge from hospital;
- Transfer to other programs such as education, vocational rehabilitation, community service club; and
- Excessive absences.

INDEPENDENT LIVING SKILL DEVELOPMENT

Purpose

To provide a small group setting within which a weekly series of shared action-situations can be used to stimulate behaviors and discussions that are directly related to the development of independent living skills; sharing responsibility for task completion, the group members will be encouraged to develop a sense of identity, competency, and efficacy in relation to themselves and others.

Rationale

The residents exhibit a resistance to attending programs outside of their immediate home-like environment. In order to provide programming, it seems most appropriate to offer a group experience on familiar territory; this is less threatening, being within the realm of their daily life patterns. A cooking program, beginning with simple group activities (such as dessert preparation for the evening meal), will facilitate engagement and the acquisition of basic group skills (decision making, communication, cohesiveness) that are essential in productive individual and group relationships and are precursors to engagement in other groups within the hospital and the community.

Patient Selection Criteria
 • Open to all residents in the cottage.

Specific Objectives
 • To improve task skills (following directions, problem solving, decision making, judgment) that will lead to successfully planning, organizing, and carrying out an activity;
 • To improve social-interpersonal skills (cooperation, sociability, responsibility); and
 • To increase familiarity with cooking techniques and terms.

Group Structure
 • Time and length of meetings: group meets once weekly for a total of 1½ hours.
 • Size of group: optimum 6.
 • Group methods and procedures:
 1. Leader initially determines task selection, breaks down task, and allocates duties.
 2. Leader serves as a role model and facilitator, engaging all members and eliciting appropriate responses.
 3. Leader allows for increasing responsibility and independence of group members with respect to task selection and completion.
 4. Patients are involved in the preparation, serving, and cleaning up of each activity.

Program Discharge Criteria
- Discharge from hospital; and
- Lack of interest and participation.

Reevaluation/Monitoring Procedures
- Observation of patients' task performance and group participation and cooperation;
- Patients' subjective comments;
- Documentation of progress toward stated group objectives and individual goals; and
- Level of functioning.

INDEPENDENT LIVING

Purpose
This is an eight-week program designed for patients who need preparation for returning to the community. It will help them to build confidence in coping with community living. People entering an independent though supervised living situation will establish or refine functional and interpersonal skills necessary for successful self-maintenance.

Goals
- Develop or improve proper self-care techniques, such as personal cleanliness, clothing repair, laundry, maintenance of living space;
- Improve money management skills, including budgeting, checking and savings accounts, use of money orders, use of sales receipts;
- Plan and prepare nutritional meals, including awareness of nutritional needs, awareness of cooking techniques, comparison shopping, use of stove, use of cookbooks, recipes and measurements, table manners;
- Improve ability to use public transportation, including map reading and personal safety factors; ·
- Assist planning and use of leisure time through the use of community resources and newspapers; and
- Increase awareness of prescribed medications and dosage.

Referral
- People who will eventually return to the community and need to practice or learn self-maintenance skills; and
- Patients who are candidates for the program will be given preference due to long-term hospitalization in accordance with grant funding recommendations.

BASIC TASK SKILLS GROUP

Purpose
This structured, basic-level group is designed as an ongoing evaluation of task skills and interpersonal behaviors. Experience in individual and group activities is used to develop and enhance work-related attitudes and skills and to practice appropriate interpersonal behavior.

Goals
- Evaluate and improve concentration;
- Evaluate and improve ability to follow directions;
- Evaluate and improve organizational skills;
- Evaluate and encourage decision making;
- Evaluate and encourage interpersonal sharing; and
- Evaluate and encourage time management.

Referrals
- Patients who require structure to perform basic tasks due to impaired concentration, temporal adaptation, and organizational skills;
- Patients experiencing difficulties making simple decisions and following simple directions;
- Patients who have difficulty performing basic tasks of daily living;
- Patients who do not participate or interact with others in group activities; and
- Patients whose functional skills demand closer evaluation.

SENSORIMOTOR PROGRAM

Purpose
To provide opportunities for gross motor activity participation; to provide opportunities for engaging in noncognitive goal-directed activity, where attention is focused on the object or outcome and the primary goal is fun; to provide opportunities for simple task involvement where the result is a concrete end product; to provide experiences ensuring success and mastery, which are thereby self-reinforcing; to facilitate socialization.

Rationale
Abnormal posture and movement patterns are often observed in the chronic schizophrenic. In a gross screening of the motivation to health population, nearly two-thirds of the patients screened exhibited behaviors suggestive of deficits related to body schema, postural balance, motor planning, and bilateral body use. Dysfunctions were also noted in learning, behavior, work, and leisure.

Sensory integrative theory postulates that these dysfunctions may be due to the inadequate organization of sensory input. In normal development, information from the various sensory receptors is used to develop basic sensorimotor patterns related to postural and reflex integration, lateralization, bilateral integration, body schema, and motor planning. These patterns enhance the development of motor skills, perceptual skills, and emotional stability, and they provide the foundation for learning and behavior.

The sensory-integrative model of personality development postulates that learned behaviors and responses, as well as adaptive interpersonal behaviors, depend on perceptual constancy (reliability of perceptual information), which ultimately depends on the integration of sensory input.

Occupational therapy treatment focuses on the facilitation of normal motor output to enhance the quality of sensory feedback. Treatment is accomplished by structuring the surroundings, materials, and demands of the environment to elicit adaptive motor responses. Adaptive responses are most readily elicited when conscious attention is focused on a purposeful activity and when mastery of the activity is attainable.

The rationale for the use of organized sensory input also stems from sensory deprivation studies. Loss of motivation, apparent in many patients, has been cited as one of the major effects of sensory deprivation. Sensory stimulation through movement-oriented activities may increase the patient's motivation for treatment and rehabilitation.

Patient Selection Criteria
- Patients exhibiting behaviors suggestive of abnormal posture and/or movement patterns;
- Withdrawn, reclusive patients who can tolerate a group setting without dangerous or destructive behavior;
- Patients whose attention span and learning capacities prevent participation in cognitive, task-oriented activities; and
- Patients who lack motivation to engage in functional activity.

Specific Treatment Objectives
- Experiencing pleasure or fun;
- Changes in affect appropriate to setting or situation;
- Increased verbalization, eye contact;
- Improved spontaneity of movement;
- Increased attention span; and
- Increased ability to follow simple instructions.

Group Structure

The program will initially consist of two 1-hour gym sessions and one swimming session per week. Enabling activities will be primarily gross motor, noncognitive, and mastery oriented, such as ballgames, tire games, rope games, mat work, parachute games, water games, floating, kicking, diving, splashing, relays, and a variety of adapted games and sports activities.

As motivation and interest improve, progression from gross motor recreational activities to highly structured task-oriented leisure activities will be pursued. Capacity, 10 patients.

Program Discharge Criteria
- Lack of tolerance for group setting;
- Excessive absences;
- Dangerous or destructive behavior; and
- Behavioral improvement indicative of the need for a higher functioning program.

Reevaluation/Monitoring Procedures

Initial baseline assessment tools include:
- Ayres clinical observations test for sensory integrative dysfunction;
- Frostig-perceptual motor battery; and
- Draw a person test.

Behavioral observations and progress note will be recorded on a regular basis.

SENSORY INTEGRATIVE PROGRAMS

Purpose

The use of movement patterns to improve information gathering and processing functions of the central nervous system and thus improve motor planning and performance behaviors.

Goals
- Improve body balance;
- Increase coordination and endurance;
- Improve awareness of self, others, and the environment;
- Decrease hypoactivity; and
- Increase joint mobility.

Referral
- Patients whose balance is impaired;
- Patients who demonstrate impaired coordination when involved in daily activities or mild physical activities;
- Patients whose activity patterns reflect hypoactivity;
- Withdrawn patients who require structure and stimulation to engage in social or functional activities;
- Patients whose endurance is low;
- Patients whose range of motion and joint mobility are limited; and
- Patients who display a tense or rigid posture or shuffling gait.

OCCUPATIONAL THERAPY SENSORIMOTOR INTEGRATION AND SCREENING GROUP

Purpose
These groups are designed to stimulate sensorimotor response, facilitate a level of response and learning readiness necessary for participation in activities, and provide functional behavior information that will make relevant and appropriate referrals possible.

Goals
- Enhance patients' ability to receive, organize, and respond to stimuli;
- Facilitate normal movement;
- Increase muscle strength and endurance;
- Improve dexterity and coordination;
- Increase energy level; and
- Increase attention span.

Referral
- Screening and improving sensorimotor response and integration;
- Patient has been rated at Level II (25–39) or higher of the Parachek Geriatric Rating Scale.
- Patient has poor gross motor and fine motor skills; and
- Patient is not oriented to time, person, or place.

OCCUPATIONAL THERAPY TASK GROUP I
(ADVANCED SENSORY-INTEGRATIVE GROUP,
PARACHEK LEVEL II/III)

Purpose
Task group I is designed to provide practice in coping with multiple sensory stimuli and gross motor skills behaviors on a performance skill level beyond the basic sensory integration groups. It will also aid in reinforcing social interaction skills as well as coping and survival skills. Group size, 12 to 15.

Goals
   • Increase ability to receive, organize, and respond to more complex stimuli;
   • Develop positive interpersonal behavior to enhance relationships with peers and authority;
   • Identify areas of self-competency and limitations;
   • Improve cognitive functioning such as memory retention, recall, sequencing, and orientation; and
   • Increase stamina.

Referral
   • Patients who have been rated at Level II (25–39) or Level III (40–50) on Parachek Geriatric Rating Scale;
   • Patient has participated in sensorimotor integration group and completed basic sensory integrative group; and
   • Patient must be able to tolerate frustration in social interaction.

OCCUPATIONAL THERAPY FUNCTIONAL
(TASK GROUP II, PARACHEK LEVEL III PATIENTS)

Purpose
This task group is designed to develop and improve task behaviors and related social and self-maintenance skills for those patients functioning at Level III as reflected on the Parachek Rating Scale.

Goals
   • Increase attention span;
   • Improve orientation and time management;
   • Enhance reality orientation;
   • Improve interactive skills of sharing, receiving, and giving;
   • Improve communication skills;
   • Increase cause-and-effect awareness; and
   • Improve fine motor skills.

- Must be oriented in at least two spheres;
- Must be able to communicate;
- Has been rated at Level III (40–50 points) on the Parachek Geriatric Rating Scale; and
- Has been referred to occupational therapy.

REALITY ORIENTATION I
(LEVEL II ON PARACHEK GERIATRIC RATING SCALE)

Purpose
This group is designed to teach and renew an orientation to time, places, and people for the older adult whose orientation has deteriorated because of long-term hospitalization, advanced age, or illness.

Goals
- Develop awareness of time as it applies to personal schedules and institutional schedule and seasonal events;
- Develop awareness of place—grounds, buildings, sleeping unit, eating place;
- Develop awareness of self in relation to others with whom one interacts; and
- Improve ability to sort out stimuli and respond appropriately.

Referral
- Patients who have deficits in reality orientation and are functioning at group Level II, Parachek Geriatric Rating Scale.

REALITY ORIENTATION II
(LEVEL III ON PARACHEK GERIATRIC RATING SCALE)

Purpose
This group is designed to upgrade orientation to time, place, and people and to make the group members aware of the outside world. Current events, politics, and hospital policies are discussed. Financial awareness is encouraged, and the surrounding environment is studied as possible sites for living. Emphasis is placed on issues relative to group living, sheltered housing, or nursing home living.

Goals
- Develop a sense of group responsibility;
- Enhance awareness of what is currently taking place outside the hospital;
- Develop some knowledge of surrounding counties as placement possibilities;
- Develop some decision-making skills; and
- Strengthen self-esteem and instill accountability for one's actions.

Referral
- Those patients who have some deficits in reality orientation but are on a Group III level of functioning on the Parachek Scale.

CAREER PREPARATION FOR WOMEN

Purpose
To provide an opportunity to explore, within a small supportive group setting, issues unique to women interested in working and finding a job. This includes relating to peers and supervisors at work, maintaining an acceptable level of job performance, and seeking and obtaining job satisfaction. The use of varied concrete activities, values clarification tasks, problem-solving situations, and role-playing exercises will be used to facilitate the development of a more realistic perception of one's assets and limitations, better management of time and personal needs.

Rationale
Within the program there are a number of female residents for whom work is a relevant topic of concern. There are many work-related issues that are unique to women and seem most appropriately addressed within a small, informal group atmosphere. These individuals show an interest in working and are currently involved in some type of vocational program. In order to provide a convenient time and setting, it seems suitable to offer a group experience immediately after work. This career preparation program will use various modalities to facilitate discussion and the acquisition of individual group skills (assertiveness, communication, friendship).

Patient Selection Criteria
- Available to meet with the group on a consistent basis;
- Willing to attend group;
- Involved in some vocational program;
- Ability to respond verbally to social contacts;
- Ability to cooperate and follow directions; and
- Interest in self-improvement.

Specific Treatment Objectives
- To improve social-interpersonal skills (cooperation, sociability, assertiveness, communication);
- To improve repertoire of responses and skills when confronted with work-related situations and issues; and
- To develop a sense of self as an effective, influential being.

Group Structure
- Time/length of meetings: group meets 3 times weekly for a total of 3 hours.
- Group size: optimum 8.
- Group Methods/Procedures

   1. Leader determines activity based on interests as expressed by group members.

   2. Leader serves as a role model and facilitator, engaging all members and contributing appropriate responses.

   3. Leader offers activities that stimulate verbal communication, allowing for interchange of feedback.

   4. Leader offers positive reinforcement and support for stated objectives.

Program Discharge Criteria
- Discharge from hospital;
- Inability to function within program criteria; and
- Transitional employment.

Reevaluation/Monitoring Procedures
- Observation of patients' participation, appearance, performance, and interactions;
- Patients' subjective comments; and
- Documentation of progress toward stated group objectives and individual goals.

JOGGING PROGRAM

Description
This is an open group that consists of men and women who will walk, jog, and exercise their way to better physical and mental health.

Goals
- To experience pleasure in moving and being outdoors;
- To improve overall physical well-being including:
  1. Cardiovascular system (health of heart and blood vessels);
  2. Greater flexibility;
  3. Weight control;
  4. Better muscle tone and strength;
  5. Increased energy; and
  6. Appearance, including figure, skin, posture, etc.
- To improve emotional well-being by
  1. Decreasing anxiety and depression; and
  2. Improving one's body image and helping to bring about a sense of mastery over one's body.
- To provide for some social participation and exchanges in a relaxed atmosphere.
- To encourage and develop self-discipline needed to participate on a consistent basis in a regularly scheduled activity.
- To have each participant gain a sense of success and satisfaction based on improvement in the above areas.
- To have participants continue to engage in this activity when on their own, in whatever setting or environment they find themselves.

Criteria
- All participants need a physician's permission to participate. This permission is based on a physical examination that would include an electrocardiograph test (EKG), blood pressure test, weight measure, and a chest X-ray.
- Seizure prone individuals should be carefully screened; those who experience them very infrequently can be included.
- Medication—any problem associated with the use of medicine should be noted by the physician and/or the psychiatrist. This should include any possible harmful side reaction, problems related to extremes in temperature, and the like.
- Clothing needed is a pair of running shoes or sneakers (as good and sturdy a pair as possible), socks, comfortable loose-fitting clothing, gloves and hat in winter, and if possible a rain jacket with hood.

PHYSICAL EXERCISE GROUP

Purpose
This activity is designed to promote a sense of physical well-being through regular participation in a structured program of physical exercise. It will provide an action-doing experience that will enable the patient to acquire a good exercise routine.

Goals
- Improve overall muscle tone, strength, endurance, flexibility, and increased efficiency of the cardiovascular system.
- Increase individual self-esteem through improved body image.
- Increase self-confidence in interpersonal interactions through participation in group activities.
- Increase awareness of the values of involvement in a physical exercise program through discussion of the positive aspects of each individual exercise.
- Promote enjoyment of physical exercise through participation in a relaxed, social atmosphere.

Referral
- Referral to the physical exercise group will cover the patient for an 8-week period; at the end of this time, patients are eligible for a renewal of referral, should this be necessary;
- Patients who demonstrate a need for specific exercises due to inactivity, weight problems, etc.;
- Patients who need to develop body awareness and improve body balance and coordination; and
- Patients who need a group that emphasizes routine discipline and physical action.

ACTIVE SPORTS

Description
This activity program provides team and individual endeavors through various sports (e.g., volleyball, basketball, softball). Team concepts are developed through practice sessions and intramural competition; opportunities for individual competition are provided through tournaments.

Goals
- Improve ability to compete an an individual and group member;
- Develop identification with a valued group;
- Improve collaborative and cooperative skills;
- Develop and maintain gross motor skills and physical endurance;
- Improve ability to handle success and failure; and
- Provide opportunity to have fun.

Criteria
- Resident of transitional program;
- Physician's written approval;
- Minimum attention span of 30 minutes;
- Tolerance of group setting;
- Ability to understand and follow 3-step directions;
- Difficulties with social-interpersonal skills; and
- Expressed interest in sports.

WALKING/HIKING PROGRAM

Description
The group is open to men and women of all ages who would like to spend two afternoons a week walking within or near the hospital grounds and occasionally at the local parks.

Goals
- To experience satisfaction and enjoyment in walking and being outdoors;
- To develop a greater appreciation of and interest in nature and the outdoors;
- To improve overall physical and mental well-being through walking and being outdoors, including:
  1. Cardiovascular functioning,
  2. Weight control,
  3. Aid to digestion and elimination,
  4. Aid to sleep,
  5. Improved appearance (posture, skin, etc.),
  6. Relaxation of tensions, and
  7. Increased energy;
- To provide opportunities to participate socially in a relaxed and pleasant environment;
- To encourage and develop self-discipline needed to participate on a consistent basis in a regularly scheduled activity; and
- To continue to participate in walking or hiking when discharged from the hospital.

Criteria

• All participants must be able to walk, at whatever pace they are able, without danger of falling.

• Participants must be in adequate physical health to walk, at their own pace, for approximately 25–45 minutes.

• All participants need a physician's approval. Individuals who are prone to seizures and those with cardiac or respiratory ailments should be carefully screened. If given permission to participate, any special limitations should be noted by the physician on the referral form.

• Any problems associated with the use of medication should be noted on the referral form by the physician or psychiatrist. This should include any possible harmful side reactions related to extremes in temperature and the like.

• Clothing should be loose, comfortable, and appropriate for the weather. Shoes should be comfortable and safe for walking.

• Only residents who are not an immediate threat to themselves or others should be considered.

BASIC LEVEL MOVEMENT GROUPS

Purpose
This group is designed for the patient who needs a highly structured movement activity. It may be used in conjunction with sensory integration activities. Opportunities are provided for the withdrawn patient to participate in movement activities within a supportive, socially reinforcing environment to stimulate response and increase the level of physical and social activity and comfort.

Goals
• Encourage body movement;
• Develop coordination;
• Develop body awareness;
• Increase attention span;
• Decrease body posturing;
• Provide opportunities to relate to others; and
• Encourage expression through movement and verbalization.

Referral Criteria
Those patients who:
• Are uncommunicative;
• Lack motivation to participate in activities;
• Have low energy level;
• Are withdrawn; and
• Are able to respond to and follow minimal directions.

GENERAL MUSIC GROUPS

Purpose
These groups are designed for the nonmusician who enjoys musical activities. Activities include sing-a-long, dance, rhythm band, musical games, record and tape listening, and some music appreciation discussion. The group allows for both verbal and nonverbal communication and active and passive participation and provides an atmosphere conducive to appropriate social behavior.

Goals
- Provide relaxation, enjoyment, and exercise;
- Provide a milieu in which appropriate social skills can be practiced;
- Offer an opportunity to express ideas and feelings;
- Improve self-esteem through musical participation;
- Counteract sedentary behavior and increase awareness and responsiveness; and
- Encourage sense of well-being.

Referral
- Open to any interested individual but may be used for specific referral if goals are appropriate;
- Should be responsive to direction and structure; and
- Those patients who need opportunity to practice or relearn social interaction skills.

SELF-EXPRESSION ART GROUP

Purpose
This group is designed to promote and improve interpersonal communication. The primary focus is on the discussion of the drawings.

Goals
- Increase ability to talk freely with peer group;
- Promote feelings of self-worth through increased ability to communicate and elicit positive feedback from group;
- Increase awareness of others and the environment;
- Increase awareness of communication as means to improve interpersonal relationships;
- Provide opportunities for creative expression; and
- Explore art as a leisure interest.

Referral
- Patients with problems in communicating;
- Patients with low self-esteem;
- Patients with poor awareness of self and environment;
- Patients with poor interpersonal skills; and
- Patients who demonstrate interest in exploring art as a leisure interest or mode for creative expression.

ALL-HOSPITAL CHORUS

Purpose
This group is designed for those patients with vocal talents and skills. Opportunities are provided for solo and chorus work. This group is structured like choruses in the community, including weekly rehearsals and occasional performances. The sessions provide an opportunity for members to relearn and practice vocal skills.

Goals
- To learn, relearn, or maintain basic vocal music skills: breathing, enunciation, phrasing, interpretations, dynamics;
- To be able to assume responsibility for care of music, attendance at rehearsals, and appropriate group and social behavior;
- To learn or relearn how to follow directions from a choral director;
- To practice performing before an audience;
- To provide opportunity to share ideas and music with group;
- To provide opportunity for interaction and group support; and
- To reexperience the pleasure of singing well and receiving approbation from others.

Referral
- Must be interested in vocal music;
- Must have some chorus or singing experience;
- Must be responsive to direction and structure; and
- Must be able to take responsibility for attendance.

CURRENT EVENTS

Purpose

This activity group is designed to increase orientation and awareness of hospital, local, state, and international events. Patients are encouraged to read newspaper articles, discuss these, and share ideas and experiences with their peers.

Goals

- Increase awareness of events occurring within the hospital and the world outside (local, state, national, international);
  - Assist patients to increase self-confidence in communication skills;
  - Increase comfort in social situations; and
  - Reinforce the enjoyment of reading newspapers and periodicals.

Referral

- Patients at an intermediate to advanced functional level;
  - Those who have an interest in or curiosity about current events;
  - Those capable of concentrating on an activity for approximately 30 minutes;
  - Patients whose social skills are not intrusive upon others; and
  - Patients whose reading ability is at grade 4 level or above.

GREENHOUSE/GARDEN GROUP

Purpose
To provide an experience that offers sensory stimulation, constructive use of leisure time, and physical exercise. This group will also facilitate the development and improvement of social, cognitive, and work skills.

Rationale
The greenhouse and garden, because of its rich sensory components and its familiar and nonthreatening elements, will encourage responsiveness, provide pleasure, and offer a connection and recall of pleasant past experiences. Nurturing plants helps orientation to time and sets a structure for attending to task.

Patient Selection Criteria
- Those who show an interest in gardening;
- Patients who are willing to attend the group and who are ambulatory; and
- Patients who exhibit one or more of the following problems:
    1. Inability or poor ability to follow directions,
    2. Poor socialization or work patterns,
    3. Poor use of leisure time, and
    4. Inability to become interested or involved in a task.

Specific Treatment Objectives
- Experience pleasure;
- Increased awareness of self and environment;
- Reinforce or improve appropriate social and work skills,
- Improved use of leisure time; and
- Improve attention span.

Group Structure
Group meets four times a week for 60–90 minutes a session; limit of 12 patients.

Program Discharge Criteria
- Discharge from hospital;
- Excessive absences;
- Social, leisure planning or task behavior; and
- Skills deficits no longer interfere with patient's functioning.

ADOLESCENT SERVICE PROGRAMS

Basic Sports—1 time/week

Purpose
Basic sports is designed to develop gross motor coordination, increase understanding of the concept of team sports, develop the concept of cooperative play, and enhance peer interactions through a small structured group. The group size is 4–6 members to allow for individual attention and instruction.

Goals
- Provide a skill base for team and individual sports;
- Promote sense of cooperative play;
- Enhance gross motor coordination; and
- Enhance peer interactions through structured team sports.

Referral
- Adolescents who need to develop basic sport skills; and
- Adolescents who need to learn how to interact and play cooperatively.

Physical Development—2 times/week

Purpose
Physical development is designed to develop or enhance body tone, endurance, flexibility, and physical body image through the use of weights, jogging, and calisthenics.

Goals
- Provide a knowledge base of physical development;
- Enhance body awareness;
- Develop physical endurance, flexibility, and body tone; and
- Increase awareness of good physical fitness.

Referral
- Adolescents who need to develop physical tone, endurance, and flexibility; and
- Adolescents who need to develop body awareness.

<u>Leisure Education—2 times/week</u>

Purpose
The leisure education program is designed to provide the opportunity for enhancement of the concept of leisure time and individual responsibility for the use of leisure time. Structured activities will be offered to aid in the understanding of the importance of developing healthy and productive leisure-time skills and in the enjoyment of such activities.

Goals
- Promote a sense of individual responsibility for one's leisure time;
- Provide a knowledge base of leisure-time skills;
- Demonstrate the importance of developing leisure-time skills in one's life;
- Provide pleasure and stimulate interest; and
- Enhance effective use of leisure time.

Referral
- Adolescents who need to develop leisure-time skills.

<u>Basic Arts and Crafts—1 time/week</u>

Purpose
Designed to develop basic arts and crafts skills, fine motor coordination, basic socialization skills, and attention span. Crafts used will be short-term and success-oriented to provide a gratifying experience.

Goals
- Develop a skill base of arts and crafts;
- Increase frustration tolerance and attention span;
- Improve fine motor coordination;
- Provide an opportunity to develop basic socialization skills; and
- Stimulate interest.

Referral
- Adolescents who need to develop frustration tolerance and attention span;
- Adolescents needing basic socialization skill development;
- Adolescents who need fine motor coordination development; and
- Adolescents who need opportunity for self-expression in a structured media.

Task Group—1 time/week

Purpose
The task group is designed to develop and enhance group cooperativeness, responsibility, and decision-making ability. Emphasis is on structured task activities designed to enhance ability to work together cooperatively and improve interpersonal relationships.

Goals
- Develop a sense of group responsibility;
- Enhance awareness of self and how one relates to others;
- Improve decision-making ability; and
- Develop and enhance organizational skills.

Referral
- Adolescents who need to improve their ability to form interpersonal relationships;
- Adolescents who need to develop group cooperative skills; and
- Adolescents who need to improve decision-making abilities.

Open Recreation—6 times/week

Purpose
Open recreation is designed to provide the opportunity for any adolescent to participate in recreation. Activities are geared toward increasing the adolescent's recreational skills, coordination, social interaction skills, and pleasure in organized play.

Goals
- Increase recreational skills;
- Provide an appropriate outlet for energies; and
- Increase ability to engage in recreational activities.

Referral
- Open.

BIBLIOGRAPHY

Allen, C. (1984). *Cognitive disabilities: Occupational therapy assessment and management.* Boston: Little Brown and Co. In Press.

American Psychiatric Association. (1982). *The young adult chronic patient.* Washington, DC: Author.

Anthony, W. A. (1980). *Principles of psychiatric rehabilitation.* Baltimore: University Park Press.

Argyris, C. (1971). *Management and organization development: The path from XA to YB.* New York: McGraw-Hill.

Argyris, C. (1982). *Reasoning, learning and action: Individual and organizational.* San Francisco: Jossey-Bass.

Austin, M. J. (1981). *Supervisory management for the human services.* Englewood Cliffs, NJ: Prentice Hall.

Austin, M. J., & Hershey, W. E. (Eds.). (1982). *Handbook on mental health administration.* San Francisco: Jossey-Bass.

Bachrach, L. L. (1980). Overview: Model programs for chronic mental patients. *American Journal of Psychiatry, 137*(9), 1023–1031.

Bachrack, S., & Lawler, E. (1980). *Power and politics in organizations: The social psychology of conflict, coalitions and bargaining.* San Francisco: Jossey-Bass.

Bennis, W. G., et al. (Eds.). (1976). *The planning of change* (3rd ed.). New York: Holt, Rinehart & Winston.

Etzioni, A. (1964). *Modern organizations.* Englewood Cliffs, NJ: Prentice Hall.

Fairweather, G. W. (1981). *The Fairweather Lodge: A twenty-five year retrospective* (New Directions for Mental Health Services Series MHS7). San Francisco: Jossey-Bass.

Feldman, S. (Ed.). (1975). *The administration of mental health services.* Springfield, IL: Charles C Thomas.

Fidler, G. S. (1982). The Life Style Performance Profile: An organizing frame. In B. J. Hemphill (Ed.), *The evaluative process in psychiatric occupational therapy* (pp. 43–47). Thorofare, NJ: Charles B. Slack.

Fidler, G. S., & Fidler, J. W. (1983). Doing and becoming: The occupational therapy experience. In G. Kielhofner (Ed.), *Health through occupation: Theory and practice in occupational therapy.* Philadelphia: F. A. Davis.

Fine, S. B. (1980). Psychiatric treatment and rehabilitation: What's in a name? *Journal of the National Association of Private Psychiatric Hospitals, 11*(5), 8–13.

Fine, S. B. (1982). *Occupational therapy: The role of rehabilitation and purposeful activity in mental health practices.* Rockville, MD: American Occupational Therapy Association.

Group for the Advancement of Psychiatry. (1982). *The positive aspects of long term hospitalization in the public sector for chronic psychiatric patients.* New York: Mental Health Materials Center.

Gunn, S. L., & Peterson, C. A. *Therapeutic recreation program design: Principles and procedures.* Englewood Cliffs, NJ: Prentice Hall.

Hersey, P., & Blanchard, K. H. (1982). *Management of organizational behavior utilizing human resources.* Englewood Cliffs, NJ: Prentice Hall.

Hospital-community treatment program for mental patients (MSU-NIMH Innovation Diffusion Project). (1978). East Lansing, MI: Michigan State University.

Hughes, P. L., & Mullins, L. (1981). *Acute psychiatric care: An occupational therapy guide to daily living skills.* Thorofare, NJ: Charles B. Slack.

Johns, E. A. (1973). *The sociology of organizational change.* New York: Pergamon Press.

Lewis, S. C. (1979). *The mature years.* Thorofare, NJ: Charles B. Slack.

Linn, M. W., et al. (1979). Day treatment and psychotropic drugs in aftercare of schizophrenic patients. *Archives of General Psychiatry, 36,* 1055–1066.

Maple, F. F. (1977). *Shared decision making.* Beverly Hills, CA: Sage Publications.

Maslin, D. (1982). Rehabilitation training for community living skills: Concepts and techniques. *Occupational Therapy in Mental Health, 2,* 33–49.

Margo, P. A., & DeSisto, M. (1983). A developmental treatment program for the chronic patient. *American Journal of Psychotherapy, 35*(1), 47–60.

Mehrabian, A. (1976). *Public places and private spaces.* New York: Basic Books.

Mintzberg, H. (1975). The manager's job: Folklore and fact. *Harvard Business Review, 8,* 49–61.

Miringoff, M. *Management in human services organizations.* New York: Macmillan.

Mollica, R. F. From asylum to community: The threatened disintegration of public psychiatry. *New England Journal of Medicine, 308*(7), 367–372.

Maslin, D. (1982). Rehabilitation training for community living skills: Concepts and techniques. *Occupational Therapy in Mental Health, 2,* 33–49.

Margo, P. A., & DeSisto, M. (1983). A developmental treatment program for the chronic patient. *American Journal of Psychotherapy, 35*(1), 47–60.

Mehrabian, A. (1976). *Public places and private spaces.* New York: Basic Books.

Mintzberg, H. (1975). The manager's job: Folklore and fact. *Harvard Business Review, 8,* 49–61.

Miringoff, M. (1980). *Management in human services organizations.* New York: Macmillan.

Mollica, R. F. From asylum to community: The threatened disintegration of public psychiatry. *New England Journal of Medicine, 308*(7), 367–372.

National Therapeutic Recreation Society. (1981). *Therapeutic recreation: An explanatory paper for the joint commission on accreditation of hospitals.* Alexandria, VA.

Okin, R. L. (1982). State hospitals in the 1980's. *Hospital and Community Psychiatry, 33*(9), 717–721.

Pepper, B., & Ryglewicz, H. (Eds.). (1982). *The young adult chronic patient* (New Directions for Mental Health Series, MHS14). San Francisco: Jossey-Bass.

Ross, M., & Burdick, D. (1981). *Sensory integration: A training manual for therapists and teachers for regressed, psychiatric and geriatric patient groups.* Thorofare, NJ: Charles B. Slack.

Schein, E. H. (1965). *Organizational psychology.* Englewood Cliffs, NJ: Prentice Hall.

Scheflen, A. E. (1982). *Levels of schizophrenia.* New York: Brunner/Mazel.

Schulberg, C. (1981). *The music therapy source book: A collection of activities categorized and analyzed.* New York: Human Sciences Press.

Spiro, H. (1982). Reforming the state hospital in a unified care system. *Hospital and Community Psychiatry, 33*(9). 722–728.

Talbot, J. A. (1978). *The death of an asylum.* New York: Grune & Stratton.

Talbot, J. A. (1981). *The chronic mentally ill.* New York: Human Sciences Press.

Wolfensberger, W. (1972). *The principle of normalization in human services.* Toronto: National Institute on Mental Retardation.

REFERENCES

American Occupational Therapy Association. (1979). *Uniform terminology for reporting occupational therapy services.* Rockville, MD: Author.

Bachrach, L. L. (1980). Overview: Model programs for chronic mental patients. *American Journal of Psychiatry, 137*(9), 1023–1031.

Baum, C. M. (1983). Management of finances, communications, personnel with resources and documentation. In H. Willard & C. Spackman (Eds.), *Occupational therapy* (pp. 815–818). New York: Lippincott.

Benne, K. O., & Birnbaum, N. (1960). Change does not have to be haphazard. *School Review, 68*(3).

Black, M. M. (1976). Adolescent role assessment. *American Journal of Occupational Therapy, 30*, 73.

Fidler, G. S. (1982). The Life Style Performance Profile: An organizing frame. In B. J. Hemphill (Ed.), *The evaluative process in psychiatric occupational therapy* (pp. 43–47). Thorofare, NJ: Charles B. Slack.

Lalonde, B. I. D. (1982). Quality assurance. In M. J. Austin & W. E. Hershey (Eds.), *Handbook on mental health administration* (pp. 352–375). San Francisco: Jossey-Bass.

Parachek, J., & King, L. J. (1976). *Parachek Geriatric Rating Scale and treatment manual.* Scottsdale, AR: Greenroom Publications.

APPENDIX

Permission to reproduce several of the following documents has been granted by:

The State of New Jersey Department of Human Services, Division of Mental Health and Hospitals for:

Rehabilitation Services Standards
Level of Functioning Assessment
Referral Form Protocol and Progress Report Form
Monthly Report Protocol and Monthly Report

Ann Langan, author, and Ancora Psychiatric Hospital for:

Activities Assessment

Charles B. Slack Inc. for:

Life Style Performance Profile, from: B. J. Hemphill, (Ed): *The evaluative process in psychiatric occupational therapy*. Thorofare, NJ, Slack Inc., © 1982. Used by permission.

State of New Jersey
Department of Human Services
Division of Mental Health and Hospitals

October 25, 1982

SUBJECT: Rehabilitation Services Standards
          Applicability: H

1. Rehabilitation Services includes those departments or contracted services whose
    primary focus is the development and restoration of those functions and performance
    skills that are essential for achieving an appropriate level of independence in
    activities of daily living and in work and leisure.

    1.1 Rehabilitation services characteristically include: Activity Therapies
         (Therapeutic Recreation, Art Therapy, Movement Therapy, Music Therapy);
         Educational Services (Academic, Consumer Health, Vocational Education);
         Occupational Therapy; Physical Therapy; Speech and Language Pathology and
         Vocational Rehabilitation.

    1.2 Such services shall be available within the facility or by a written contract
         with an individual or agency outside of the facility.

2. Rehabilitation Services shall have written policies and procedures that address the
    over-all philosophy, goals and organizational procedures of rehabilitation services.

    2.1 Each department/service shall have a written plan that describes its organization,
         philosophy, goals, policies, and functions.

    2.2 Clear, measureable goals and objectives shall be written for each department/
         service, and there shall be a documented process for monitoring goal attainment.

    2.3 Rehabilitation Services shall have a qualified professional responsible for the
         coordination, management, and over-all direction of services who is currently
         credentialed in one of the rehabilitation specialties.

    2.4 Each department or service within Rehabilitation Services shall be headed by a
         qualified professional currently credentialed in the respective professional
         field.

3. Rehabilitation Services must be an integral, high priority part of patient care
    services.

    3.1 Rehabilitation Services must have a direct line of authority to the management
         and decision making bodies of the institution.

    3.2 Rehabilitation staff shall hold membership in appropriate administrative and
         clinical committees.

    3.3 There must be documented evidence of functional linkage with clinical services
         and the treatment teams.

    3.4 Participation in and collaboration with the treatment team shall be sufficient
         to ensure comprehensive treatment planning and regular progress review.

4. Departments within rehabilitation services shall have appropriate linkage with
    resources and services outside the institution and a well organized plan for using
    and collaborating with such resources.

5. Rehabilitation Services must be integrated. Program design and the manner in which
    program is implemented shall reflect inter-departmental program sharing and
    collaboration so that the patient's educational, social, physical, psychological,
    recreational and vocational needs are addressed in an integrated and developmentally
    sequenced manner.

6. Program services must be comprehensive.

    6.1 Services for patients shall offer remediation programs that are specifically
         designed to address the following problems and are accessible to all patients
         requiring such services.

Impairment in sensory integration and perception.

Physical disabilities and debilitation.

Impairments and deficits in task behaviors and cognitive skills.

Deficiencies in the ability to play and to experience pleasure.

Limitations in social and interpersonal skills.

Speech, language, and hearing disorders and impairments.

Deficiencies in work habits, attitudes, and skills.

Learning disabilities and educational deficiencies.

Limitations in self care and self maintenance skills.

6.2 Program design and organization shall be based on current Level of Function (LOF) data of the hospital population.

7. Services for patients must be individualized. They shall reflect a personally tailored, integrated regimen, clearly designed and adjusted to the individual's level of functioning and specific rehabilitation problems and needs as these are specified in the Discharge Oriented Service Plan (DOSP).

7.1 There shall be a written statement defining the specific rehabilitation goals and objectives of each program or activity offered by a department or service.

7.2 Programs must be culturally and economically relevant and shall be congruent with the patient's past and anticipated life style and social role.

7.3 The kinds of activities provided and the context in which they occur shall conform to and reflect cultural and economic realities of the individual patient and the environment.

7.4 Program schedules and daily routines shall reflect a culturally relevant, age appropriate, normal use of time with appropriate tasks and activities. The kinds of programs and the times at which they are offered shall reflect a normal life style of appropriately timed work, leisure, and rest.

7.5 Recreation, socialization, library services, adult education, and other appropriate activities shall be available to all patients during evenings and on weekends.

7.6 Special holiday programs shall be accessible to all patients on the day on which the holiday occurs.

7.7 As appropriate, patients shall play an active role in planning and implementing their leisure programs.

7.8 There shall be a well organized, written plan for the regular review and revision of programs and services to ensure that programs are relevant to the level of functioning, the culture, and the needs and interests of patients.

7.9 There shall be written procedures for on-going patient care monitoring activities and for review of the utilization of rehabilitation resources.

8. There shall be an adequate number of appropriately qualified staff to provide the needed services to monitor programs and adequately supervise assistive staff.

8.1 There shall be a clearly designed table of organization and plan to ensure adequate and appropriate on-going supervision of both professional and paraprofessional staff.

8.2 Documentation shall verify that supervision is on-going and provides the essential and appropriate professional counsel and guidance to staff in the areas of direct patient services and the management of such services.

8.3 There shall be documentation to verify that professional staff are credentialed in the appropriate field.

8.4 There shall be an adequate number of Qualified Occupational Therapy staff to provide the following programs for all patients for whom such remediation is indicated:

Training in activities of daily living
Sensory integration
Physical restoration
Pre-vocational assessment and training
Task skills development
Social and leisure skill development

8.5 There shall be an adequate number of qualified Activity Therapy staff to provide the following programs, as appropriate to the needs of patients:

Evening, week-end and holiday recreation
Leisure interest and skill development
Physical fitness training
Music, movement, art therapy
Socialization programs

8.6 There shall be an adequate number of qualified Vocational Rehabilitation staff to provide the following, as appropriate to the needs of patients:

Vocational testing, evaluation, and assessment
Work skills training programs
On-the-job training programs
Work and job placement
Vocational counseling

8.7 There shall be an adequate number of qualified Education staff to provide the following, as appropriate to the needs of patients:

Academic education
Remedial education
Health education
Vocational education

8.8 Qualified Physical Therapy staff or contracted services shall be adequate to provide the following physical therapy services, readily accessible to all patients needing such services:

Mobility and ambulation training
Physical restoration to include:
    Muscle and joint facilitation
    Orthotics and prosthetics
    Wheel chair management

8.9 Qualified Speech and Language staff or contracted services shall be adequate to provide the following services, readily accessible to all patients requiring such services:

Speech, language and hearing screening and assessments
Remedial programs for language development
Communication skills training
Assistive devise training and use

9. Assessments and evaluations shall be adequate for establishing rehabilitation goals, setting priorities, monitoring progress, and planning discharge.

9.1 An initial rehabilitation needs assessment shall be completed on all patients admitted to the facility. This assessment shall be completed within 10 calendar days of admission and shall include an overview of:

Education: current and past interests, abilities, and achievements
Work history: current and past skills, interests, attitudes, and motivation
Leisure skills: current and past interests, abilities, and leisure patterns
Physical functioning: abilities, aptitudes, disabilities, and limitations.
To include speech/hearing limitations or disabilities
Social: attitudes, skills, and behaviors
Self maintenance: skills, deficits, and patterns
Life style: daily activity patterns
Recommendations for program focus, specific intervention strategies, and/or further evaluations.

9.2 An occupational therapy evaluation shall be completed on all patients referred to that service. Such evaluation shall include, as appropriate to goals and problems, in-depth assessments of:

Sensory-motor integration, perception
Physical functioning
Task behaviors, cognitive skills
Self maintenance skills, limitations
Interpersonal and group skills and behaviors
Leisure interests and patterns
Activity configuration summary
Recommendations for goal focus and priorities

9.3 A vocational rehabilitation assessment shall be completed on all patients referred to that service and shall include in-depth information relative to:

Vocational history
Work skills and aptitudes
Work skill deficits and training needs
Work attitudes, habits, interests, and motivations
Interest in and potential for training and/or practice
Recommendations for programming and priority focus

9.4 Comprehensive speech, language and hearing evaluations shall be provided when initial screening and/or performance behaviors indicate a deficiency or dysfunction in communication.

9.5 Standardized, educational assessments and an Individual Education Plan shall be completed or updated on all patients 21 years of age and younger.

9.5.1 Such assessments and plans shall meet the requirements of the State, Federal and local school districts.

9.5.2 Adult patients referred to education services shall be assessed as appropriate and learning goals established in concert with treatment goals.

9.6 An in-depth assessment of the patient's leisure interests, skills and aptitudes; social and interpersonal behaviors and skills; communication patterns, style and needs shall be completed in response to a referral for therapeutic recreation, music, art or movement therapy. Such assessments shall include recommendations for future treatment goal focus.

10. A written signed referral from the treatment team is necessary for the initiation of any rehabilitation service, except for open recreation programs.

10.1 A referral is not required for participation in open recreation and socialization activities such as those provided for general fun, relaxation, and normalization.

10.1.1 Some means of documenting participation in such programs shall be evident.

11. A progress note at the required intervals shall be documented in the clinical record for each patient for whom a referral to a rehabilitation service has been made.

11.1 A discharge summary note shall be completed at the time of discharge from or discontinuation of a service or program. Such a note shall include a summary of progress in relation to the goal(s) that were established; a statement of current status; and as appropriate, recommendations for continued and/or other programs or services.

12. There shall be an established, written procedure and formula for making budgetary allocations to rehabilitation services, to the departments or programs within Rehabilitation and a mechanism for monitoring expenditures.

12.1 Rehabilitation Services/departments shall be involved in the process of allocating funds for rehabilitation.

12.2 A specific amount of money shall be allocated to Rehabilitation Services on a yearly basis.

12.3 There shall be a clearly defined procedure for regularly providing accounting statements of expenditures and balances.

13. Record keeping shall be adequate for tracking referrals and discharges, verifying attendance and schedules, auditing utilization of services, monitoring and recording patient earnings, and such other data as are required for the operation of services and quality assurance.

    13.1 All patient work programs shall conform to State and Federal wage and hour regulations.

14. Rehabilitation services shall maintain on-going staff development programs.

    14.1 Rehabilitation staff shall receive training and demonstrate competence in handling medical and psychiatric emergencies.

    14.2 Engagement in continuing education, professional affiliations, and advanced education and research shall be supported and encouraged.

15. Appropriate space, equipment, and facilities shall be provided.

    15.1 All space, equipment and facilities shall meet Federal, State and local requirements for safety, fire prevention, health and sanitation.

Adapted from:

Fidler, Gail S., Design of Rehabilitation Services in Psychiatric Hospital Settings, RAMSCO Publications, Maryland 1984.

Consolidated Standards, JCAH, 1981.

Richard H. Wilson, Director
Division of Mental Health and Hospitals

<table>
<tr><td colspan="2">

Client Identification

Use Addressograph in space at right.

If no Addressograph available, write in:

name (optional), case number, and date
of this admission.

</td><td></td></tr>
<tr><td></td><td>Case #</td><td>Mo/Yr Adm. Date</td></tr>
</table>

LEVEL OF FUNCTIONING ASSESSMENT (LOF)

RATER INFORMATION	CLIENT INFORMATION
Name of Hospital or Community Agency:_____ /_____ (Code) Name of Ward or Program Unit:_____ /_____ (Code) Name of Rater:_____ (please print) Date of which this form was filled out: / / / / / (Month) (Day) (Year) Date of last Level of Functioning Assessment: / / / / / (Month) (Day) (Year) Is this Assessment being made at (circle one): Admission, Follow-up, Transfer, or Discharge?	Unique Client ID Number:__ __ __ __ __ __ __ Date of Birth: / / / / / Month Day Year Sex: ___M ___F Home Address:_____ (Municipality) Is this person currently here on Court Detainer? _____Yes _____No Does this person have family members living nearby? _____Yes _____No Is this person able to speak English fluently? _____Yes _____No If No, what language does the person ordinarily speak? _____ Specify

On the following pages you will be asked to make some judgments about this client's skills
and abilities. Please remember that your answers should reflect what has been most typical
of the client during the past week, the way the client has been most of the time.
Therefore, do not limit your rating only to the way the client was the last time you saw
him/her. Your rating will have a great deal to do with the service this person will
receive, so it is essential that you use your knowledge of the client's usual condition
during the past week.

Base your answers on how persons of similar age, sex, and general background manage these
activities in normal daily living. Do not use your program or facility as your only basis
for comparison. We are less interested in how well someone has adjusted to your program
than we are in how well he/she could manage outside it.

Above all, use common sense. These items are not too technical or complex, and you
should use the best information and best judgment you can in making the assessment.

Instructions: Circle the number that best describes this person's <u>typical</u> level of functioning on each item listed below. BE AS ACCURATE AS YOU CAN. If you are not sure about a certain rating, ask someone who might know or consult the case record.

MARK ONLY ONE NUMBER FOR EACH ITEM. BE SURE TO MARK ALL ITEMS.

SELF MAINTENANCE				
A. Physical Functioning	NO PROBLEM	PROBLEM, BUT NO EFFECT ON GENERAL FUNCTIONING	SLIGHT EFFECT ON GENERAL FUNCTIONING	RESTRICTS GENERAL FUNCTIONING SUBSTANTIALLY	PREVENTS GENERAL FUNCTIONING
1. VISION	5	4	3	2	1
2. HEARING	5	4	3	2	1
3. SPEECH IMPAIRMENT	5	4	3	2	1
4. WALKING, USE OF LEGS	5	4	3	2	1
5. USE OF HANDS AND ARMS	5	4	3	2	1
B. Personal Care Skills	TOTALLY SELF-SUFFICIENT	NEEDS VERBAL ADVICE OR GUIDANCE	NEEDS SOME PHYSICAL HELP OR ASSISTANCE	NEEDS SUBSTANTIAL HELP	TOTALLY DEPENDENT
6. TOILETING (Uses toilet properly; keeps self and area clean)	5	4	3	2	1
7. EATING (uses utensils properly; eating habits)	5	4	3	2	1
8. PERSONAL HYGIENE (body and teeth; general cleanliness)	5	4	3	2	1
9. DRESSING SELF (selects appropriate garments; dresses self)	5	4	3	2	1
10. GROOMING (hair, make-up, general appearance)	5	4	3	2	1
11. CARE OF OWN POSSESSIONS	5	4	3	2	1
12. CARE OF OWN LIVING SPACE	5	4	3	2	1
SOCIAL FUNCTIONING				
C. Interpersonal Relationships	HIGHLY TYPICAL OF THIS PERSON	GENERALLY TYPICAL OF THIS PERSON	SOMEWHAT TYPICAL OF THIS PERSON	GENERALLY UNTYPICAL OF THIS PERSON	HIGHLY UNTYPICAL OF THIS PERSON
13. ACCEPTS CONTACT WITH OTHERS (does not withdraw or turn away)	5	4	3	2	1
14. INITIATES CONTACT WITH OTHERS	5	4	3	2	1
15. COMMUNICATES EFFECTIVELY (speech and gestures are understandable and to the point)	5	4	3	2	1
16. ENGAGES IN ACTIVITIES WITHOUT PROMPTING	5	4	3	2	1
17. PARTICIPATES IN GROUPS	5	4	3	2	1
18. FORMS AND MAINTAINS FRIENDSHIPS	5	4	3	2	1
19. ASKS FOR HELP WHEN NEEDED	5	4	3	2	1

D. Social Acceptability	NEVER	RARELY	SOMETIMES	FREQUENTLY	ALWAYS
20. VERBALLY ABUSES OTHERS	5	4	3	2	1
21. PHYSICALLY ABUSES OTHERS	5	4	3	2	1
22. DESTROYS PROPERTY	5	4	3	2	1
23. PHYSICALLY ABUSES SELF	5	4	3	2	1
24. IS FEARFUL, CRYING, CLINGING	5	4	3	2	1
25. TAKES PROPERTY FROM OTHERS' WITHOUT PERMISSION	5	4	3	2	1
26. PERFORMS REPETITIVE BEHAVIORS (pacing, rocking, making noises, etc.)	5	4	3	2	1

COMMUNITY LIVING SKILLS

E. Activities	TOTALLY SELF-SUFFICIENT	NEEDS VERBAL ADVICE OR GUIDANCE	NEEDS SOME PHYSICAL HELP OR ASSISTANCE	NEEDS SUBSTANTIAL HELP	TOTALLY DEPENDENT
27. HOUSEHOLD RESPONSIBILITIES (house cleaning, cooking, washing clothes, etc.)	5	4	3	2	1
28. SHOPPING (selection of items, choice of stores,	5	4	3	2	1
29. HANDLING PERSONAL FINANCES (budgeting, paying bills)	5	4	3	2	1
30. USE OF TELEPHONE (getting number, dialing, speaking, listening)	5	4	3	2	1
31. TRAVELING FROM RESIDENCE WITHOUT GETTING LOST	5	4	3	2	1
32. USE OF PUBLIC TRANSPORTA-TION (selecting route, using timetable, paying fares, making transfers)	5	4	3	2	1
33. USE OF LEISURE TIME (reading, visiting friends, listening to music, etc.)	5	4	3	2	1
34. RECOGNIZING AND AVOIDING COMMON DANGERS (traffic safety, fire safety, etc.)	5	4	3	2	1
35. SELF-MEDICATION (understanding purpose, taking as prescribed, recognizing side effects)	5	4	3	2	1
36. USE OF MEDICAL AND OTHER COMMUNITY SERVICES (knowing who to contact, how, and when to use.)	5	4	3	2	1
37. BASIC READING, WRITING, AND ARITHMETIC (enough for daily needs)	5	4	3	2	1

F. Work Skills	HIGHLY TYPICAL OF THIS PERSON	GENERALLY TYPICAL OF THIS PERSON	SOMEWHAT TYPICAL OF THIS PERSON	GENERALLY UNTYPICAL OF THIS PERSON	HIGHLY UNTYPICAL OF THIS PERSON
38. HAS EMPLOYABLE SKILLS	5	4	3	2	1
39. WORKS WITH MINIMAL SUPERVISION	5	4	3	2	1
40. IS ABLE TO SUSTAIN WORK EFFORT (not easily distracted; can work under stress)	5	4	3	2	1
41. APPEARS AT APPOINTMENTS ON TIME	5	4	3	2	1
42. FOLLOWS VERBAL INSTRUCTIONS ACCURATELY	5	4	3	2	1
43. COMPLETES ASSIGNED TASKS	5	4	3	2	1

OTHER INFORMATION

44. From your knowledge of this person, are there other skills or problem areas not covered on this form that are important to this person's ability to function independently? If so, please specify.

_____

_____

_____

_____

_____

45. How well do you know the skills and behavior of the person you just rated? (Circle one)

VERY WELL		FAIRLY WELL		NOT VERY WELL AT ALL
5	4	3	2	1

46. Have you discussed this assessment with the client? (Circle one)

    Yes   No

If YES, does the client generally agree with the assessment? (Circle one)

    Yes   No

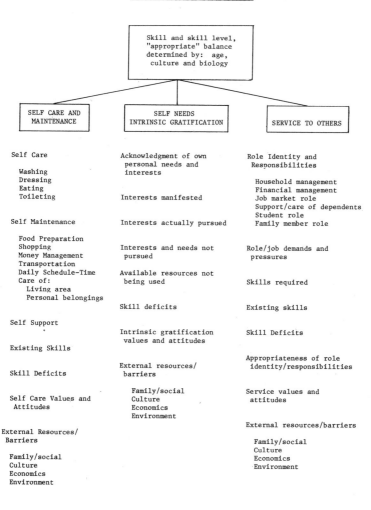

LIFE STYLE PERFORMANCE PROFILE

```
                        ┌─────────────────────────┐
                        │  Skill and skill level, │
                        │  "appropriate" balance  │
                        │  determined by:  age,   │
                        │  culture and biology    │
                        └─────────────────────────┘
```

SELF CARE AND MAINTENANCE	SELF NEEDS INTRINSIC GRATIFICATION	SERVICE TO OTHERS

Self Care

    Washing
    Dressing
    Eating
    Toileting

Self Maintenance

    Food Preparation
    Shopping
    Money Management
    Transportation
    Daily Schedule-Time
    Care of:
        Living area
        Personal belongings

Self Support

Existing Skills

Skill Deficits

Self Care Values and
Attitudes

External Resources/
Barriers

    Family/social
    Culture
    Economics
    Environment

Acknowledgment of own
personal needs and
interests

Interests manifested

Interests actually pursued

Interests and needs not
pursued

Available resources not
being used

Skill deficits

Intrinsic gratification
values and attitudes

External resources/
barriers

    Family/social
    Culture
    Economics
    Environment

Role Identity and
Responsibilities

    Household management
    Financial management
    Job market role
    Support/care of dependents
    Student role
    Family member role

Role/job demands and
pressures

Skills required

Existing skills

Skill Deficits

Appropriateness of role
identity/responsibilities

Service values and
attitudes

External resources/barriers

    Family/social
    Culture
    Economics
    Environment

GREYSTONE PARK PSYCHIATRIC HOSPITAL

ACTIVITY INTEREST PROFILE

Name: Date:

Building: Ward:

On the reverse side is a list of leisure time activities. Please indicate in the
appropriate column your past, current, and future interests.

Activity	Past Experience	Current Participation	Would Like to Learn or Relearn
Participatory Sports			
Table Games			
Arts & Crafts Activities			
Spectator Activities			
Creative Arts Activities			

Resident's signature_____

Staff signature_____

Participatory Sports

Badminton
Baseball
Basketball
Bowling
Croquet
Exercises
Football
Horseshoes
Ice Skating
Jogging
Ping Pong
Pool
Roller Skating
Soccer
Swimming
Tennis
Volleyball

Table Games

Backgammon
Bingo
Cards
Checkers
Chess
Puzzles

Arts and Crafts Activities

Ceramics
Crocheting
Decoupage
Drawing
Embroidery
Knitting
Macrame
Mosaics
Painting
Sewing
Weaving
Woodworking

Spectator Activities

Ballet
Concerts
Movies
Museums
Opera
Sports events
Theater, plays
Zoos

Creative Arts Activities

Acting
Creative writing
Dancing (Social Dancing)
Discussion groups
Listening to Music
Musical instrument (playing)
Poetry
Reading
Singing

ANCORA PSYCHIATRIC HOSPITAL
ACTIVITIES ASSESSMENT

CODE:
S-Strong
C-Casual
No-None

I. INTEREST CHECKLIST

Please check each item below according to your interest.

ACTIVITY	INTEREST	ACTIVITY	INTEREST	ACTIVITY	INTEREST

Hobbies, Arts, Crafts   S C No

- Sewing
- Woodworking
- Model Building
- Needlework
- Knitting
- Crochet
- Leatherwork
- Pottery &
  Ceramics
- Collecting
- Photography
- Painting
- Drawing
- Other

Music and Dance*

- Music Listening
- Singing
- Piano
- Guitar
- Drums
- Group Singing
- Dance
- Other

Community Trips

- Museums
- Concerts
- Sports Events
- Movies
- Historical
  Sites
- Boardwalk
- Theatre/Plays
- Eating Out
- Other

Sports/Outdoor Activities*   S C No

- Baseball
- Basketball
- Volleyball
- Football
- Golf
- Shuffleboard
- Ping Pong
- Billiards
- Badminton
- Tennis
- Swimming
- Exercise
- Jogging
- Nature Walks
- Picnic/
  Barb-B-Q
- Gardening
- Fishing
- Other

Table Games

- Puzzles
- Cards
- Bingo
- Solitaire
- Chess
- Checkers
- Dominoes
- Backgammon
- Scrabble
- Monopoly
- Parchesi
- Other

Educational Interests   S C No

- Languages
- Writing
- Debates
- Reading
- Slides/
  Discussions
- Social Studies
- Math
- History
- Science
- Consumer Info
- Other

Home Activities

- Ironing
- Mending
- Cooking
- Shopping
- Housekeeping
- Laundry
- Indoor
  Gardening
- Home Decorating
- Television
- Other

Social Activities

- Visiting
  Friends
- Parties
- Letter writing
- Family
  Get-together
- Culture Interest
  groups
- Committee work
- Church activities
- Service groups
- Residents
  Council
- Other

*Indicate active or passive (listening/watching) participation.

Resident's involvement in providing above information_____

_____

_____

UNIT: WARD:

ACTIVITIES ASSESSMENT

II. <u>SKILLS AND INTERESTS</u>

Abilities/Aptitudes/Talents _____

Prior Work Experiences _____

Favorite Past-Times/Hobbies _____

Homemaker Skills/Interests _____

Current Time Utilization/Daily Routine _____

Plan for Use of Time after Discharge _____

    Work: _____

    Home/Living: _____

    Leisure/Social: _____

III. <u>FACTORS AFFECTING ACTIVITIES PROGRAM PARTICIPATION</u>

Physical _____

Cognitive _____

Emotional _____

IV. <u>NEEDS TO BE ADDRESSED/PROGRAM RECOMMENDATION</u>

Physical _____

Psychosocial _____

Daily Life Skills _____

    Work/School: _____

    Home: _____

    Leisure/Social: _____

_____
Date

_____
Signature and Title

Guidelines for the ACTIVITIES ASSESSMENT Form

I. Interest Checklist

The Interest Checklist is completed by staff in interview with the patient. The
patient is asked to what extent, if any, he is interested in the activities listed.
Comment shall be made on the patient's ability or cooperation in providing this
information.

Comment should also be made on the type of participation the patient indicates in
these activities, i.e. whether he enjoys "watching" sports as a passive observer,
or is interested in active participation; whether he "used to be" interested or
would prefer to try a new activity presently.

If Interest Checklist cannot be completed, indicate the reason why. Also comment
on the accuracy of the patient's responses, if you feel that he is not providing
thoughtful or reflective or true responses to your questions.

II. Skills and Interests

This section is completed by staff. Information can be gleaned from: 1. the
patient, 2. the clinical record, 3. staff who have observed the patient, 4. direct
observation of the patient by the assessor.

Abilities/Aptitudes/Talents

Skills, training, strong interests, experiences, hobbies which may comprise
strengths for the patient should be listed here.

Ask the patient for the following:

What are your best abilities or talents?
What do you feel you do well?
What special training have you had?
What would you like to be able to do in the hospital that uses your abilities?
What do you like to do that you have gained skill or experience in?

Prior Work Experience

What jobs have you had?
When did you last work?
What schooling have you had?
What do you like about work?
What were you best in in your work?
When were you happiest in your life?
What were you doing then?

Favorite Pastimes/Hobbies

What do you especially like to do?
What hobbies do you have?
What clubs, churches, organizations did you belong to?
What did you do during vacation or during free time?
When was the favorite happiest time in your life?
What were you doing then?
How was it a good time?
What activities would you like to do more?

We offer some activities here for patients. (Explain to the patient which
activities are offered.)
Would you enjoy doing any of these?

111

<u>Homemaker Skills/Interests</u>

What kinds of things must you do to be able to manage at home?
Where will you be discharged to?
What kinds of skills do you need to manage well in that situation?
Do you feel comfortable about being able to manage at home (or other discharge
situation)?
What skills do you feel you need to learn?

Note: Staff should comment on patient's self maintenance skills against the
expectation of his present and excepted living situation.

<u>Current Time Utilization</u>

Comment on work/home (self-maintenance)/ social/ leisure/ rest aspects of the
patient's time utilization currently.
How does the patient use his time during the day? What would the patient have to
do to gain more satisfaction from his daily activities? How does he feel about
this? Is there an imbalance in the patient's activities/rest daily pattern?
Does he feel that he is lacking satisfaction in his daily routine? Does he know
what he needs more or less of?

<u>Plan for Use of Time After Discharge</u>

Does the patient feel that he needs to make changes in order to live a more
satisfying life after discharge? Or does he blame hospitalization on others?
What will he do that is different when he is discharged that will perhaps lead to
greater satisfaction? If self medication has been a problem, what are his
intentions in this regard? If withdrawal or lack of social stimulation has been
a problem, what steps does the patient plan to take to rectify this? How can
hospital staff help prepare him for discharge and anxiety associated with it?

If imbalance of work, social, leisure, home activities has been a problem,
how can the patient begin to recognize and deal with or plan to reduce this
imbalance?

What would he have to do to gain more satisfaction in his daily activities? How
does he feel about this? Comment on work, home, social, leisure aspects of his
life pattern after discharge.

III. <u>Factors Affecting Activities Program Participation</u>

1. Physical abilities/limitations

   Look for, and comment on selectively:

        -medical precautions such as cardiac, seizure, diabetes, etc.
        -confinement to wheel chair, bed/geri chair
        -sensory skills/limitations i.e. hearing, touch, vision
        -motor skills/limitations, including posture, balance, endurance
        -spontaneous reactions and reflexes, gross/fine motor coordination
        -eye-hand coordination, manual dexterity, perceptual motor skills

2. Cognitive

   Look for and comment on selectively:

        -attention span
        -orientation to time, place, person and activity
        -ability to perform familiar activities
        -needs demonstration to learn new activities
        -requires simple directions to learn new activities
        -ability to follow multi-step directions in activities
        -learns new and complex activities quickly
        -can problem solve independently
        -can concentrate for duration of activity
        -can concentrate despite distractions
        -can organize a complex activity, i.e. plan, understand, perform
        -is able to perform wide variety of activities
        -is self-directed in unstructured setting in choice of activity and
            participation
        -comment on memory, short and long term
        -soundness of judgment in performing activities

3. Emotional (including social)

Look for and comment on selectivity:

-demonstration of awareness of others' needs/feelings
-cooperation with task, group, staff or situational expectations
-spontaneous clear appropriate expression of affect
-comfort level with initiating and/or responding to verbal instruction
-good sportsmanship, both in winning and losing
-comfort level as group participant
-(affective) acceptance of authority
-ability to recognize, verbalize and act on needs and feelings
-ability to experience and express enjoyment in activities
-ability to express self thru creative activities (music, art, poetry, dance)
-motivation/interest level for activities
-personal satisfaction derived from participation in activities
-experiences/expresses frustration with specific activities
-tolerates activity briefly with low frustration tolerance
-performs activities with angry or destructive motions or verbalization
-approaches all activities in an angry, aggressive manner

IV. Needs to be Addressed/Program Recommendations

Summarize the patient's physical, psychosocial or daily life skills/needs that can be addressed through activities program participation.

Suggest ways to use patient's strengths to meet needs.

Refer to Guide for Activities and Recreation Programs for referral for examples of needs which can be addressed through these services.

Recommend specific activities/services offered through rehabilitation or other hospital services.

Rehabilitation Services

I. Referral Form Protocol

The Rehabilitation Referral Form is to be used by the treatment team in making a referral to any of the Rehabilitation Services. The Referral form will serve to communicate the treatment team's request for Rehabilitation Service and to initiate specific action. As stated on the Referral Form, a separate referral document is to be used for each service being requested for each client. The goals stated on the referral form must reflect and correspond to the goals stated in the individual treatment plan (DOSP). Both the Treatment plan and the multidisciplinary progress notes must document that such a referral has been initiated. The referral form is to be forwarded to the appropriate Rehabilitation Services Department for processing and follow-up.

In case of a patient's SELF REFERRAL the particular Rehabilitation Service staff will generate a Reporting Form which will be sent to the treatment team for consideration and appropriate action.

The referral is to be kept by the appropriate department until the service has been completed, discontinued or changed. The original referral is then returned to the treatment team coordinator (or case manager) with a final summary.

If the referral cannot be acted upon immediately, is incomplete or is deemed inappropriate, it is to be returned to the treatment team coordinator or case manager with appropriate notation and/or request for clarification or additional information.

II. Progress Report Form

The Rehabilitation Services Progress Report Form is to be used for documenting an initial referral response, on-going monthly progress, recommendations for alternatives or changes in goals, and a discharge summary. All Progress Reports are to be forwarded to the appropriate case manager or treatment team coordinator to be entered in the patient's medical chart.

A response to an initial referral will be generated on this form within five (5) days of receipt of the referral. Such a response may simply acknowledge that the referral has been received with an indication of when the referral will be implemented or it may summarize actions taken and findings resulting from the referral.

An initial note is to be recorded on this form and forwarded within five (5) working days after the patient has been seen.

Monthly progress notes are to be sent five working days before the end of each month.

A discharge summary is to be completed within five (5) working days after the patient has left the program.

114

State of New Jersey
Department of Human Services
Division of Mental Health and Hospitals

Rehabilitation Services

Referral Form

Client Identification

Use Addressograph in space at right. If no
Addressograph available, write in: name,
unit, date of admission, sex and date of birth.

(Check Appropriate Service)

Education	_____	Vocational Rehabilitation	_____
Occupational Therapy	_____	Therapeutic Recreation	_____
Physical Therapy	_____	Music Therapy	_____
Speech/Language Pathology	_____	Movement Therapy	_____
		Art Therapy	_____

Reason for referral:_____

_____

_____
Evaluate, Re-assess, Program Plan

Treatment Goals:_____

_____

_____

_____

_____

_____

Restrictions/Limitations and Privileges:_____

_____

_____

_____

Referred by:_____ Unit:_____ Date:_____

Instructions:

1. Use a separate form for referral to each service and for each patient.

2. The goals stated on the referral must correspond to the goals of the Individual
    Treatment Plan (DOSP).

3. Return this referral when service is completed, discontinued or when new goals are
    established by the treatment team.

115

State of New Jersey
Department of Human Services
Division of Mental Health and Hospitals

Rehabilitation Services

Progress Report Form

NAME_____   UNIT & WARD_____

Check Types of Report

INITIAL REFERRAL   MONTHLY PROGRESS   DISCHARGE SUMMARY
     NOTE:_____   NOTE:_____   NOTE:_____

_____

_____

_____

_____

_____

_____

_____

_____

_____

_____

_____

Recommendations:_____

_____

_____

_____

_____

Program Assignment:_____

Anticipated Duration of Participation:_____

Scheduled Time:_____

_____   _____
    (Signature/Title of Rehabilitation Specialist)   Date

Instructions:

1.   Send all notes to the case manager or designee.

2.   Send a response note to the initial referral within 5 days.

3.   Send the initial note within 5 days after patient has been seen.

4.   Send monthly progress notes 5 working days before end of each month.

Goals and Objectives

(Narrative Format)

SERVICES DEPARTMENT

NAME OF PROJECT: DEVELOP SCHEDULE AND REVIEW AND REVISE ACTIVITY RELATED PROGRAM
                 PROCEDURES, DIRECTIVES, AND PROGRAM GUIDE

GOAL#10 Compliance JCAH Contingencies and toward a DOSP System

WHAT WILL BE DONE   .

        Develop time frame
        Review and revise

HOW IT WILL BE DONE

        Following Administration Procedure #001 and R.S. Directive #1 review and revise
        prior administrative reviews of department procedures (May of each year)

WHO IS GOING TO DO THIS

        Activities Coordinator - Procedures and Directives
        Activity Staff - Program Guide during bi-monthly in-service time

WHEN WILL IT BE ACCOMPLISHED

        April of each year   RS Procedures #403 Activity Program
                              RD Directives 4, 12, 18, 20, 22, 25, 30, 33, 38, 39,
                                            52, 53, 55
        March   Program Guide
MEASURE TO INDICATE THAT THE PROJECT HAS BEEN COMPLETED OR TO WHAT DEGREE

        Timely completion
        Consistency with DOSP system
JANUARY 1983
        _____

NAME OF PROJECT: ADD STATISTICAL DISCUSSION TO MONTHLY REPORT

GOAL#10 Compliance to JCAH Contingencies; Examine Utilization of staff & Services –
        monthly, yearly

WHAT WILL BE DONE

        Provide a base from which to perform yearly program evaluation
        Examine resident involvement, use of staff time

HOW IT WILL BE DONE

        Current statistical information will be compared to month(s) prior, noting
        fluctations, program and staff changes and impact of other program

WHO IS GOING TO DO THIS

        Coordinator of Activities Department

WHEN WILL IT BE ACCOMPLISHED

        Monthly starting January 1983, with a yearly computation in December 1983

MEASURE TO INDICATE THAT THE PROJECT HAS BEEN COMPLETED OR TO WHAT DEGREE

        Monthly report to include statistical discussion
        Yearly evaluation to utilize monthly statistics

JANUARY 1982

NAME OF PROJECT: DOSP IMPLEMENTATION

GOAL # 1

WHAT WILL BE DONE

> Implementation of documentation of Work Activities progress notes. To review
> the treatment plans of all residents currently participating in Work Activities
> is listed as a treatment team objective.

HOW IT WILL BE DONE

> A tickler system will be set up on all residents into two sections, those
> that participate and those that do not participate. A review of each
> residents chart will be made of those participating at present.

WHO IS GOING TO DO THIS

> The Work Activities Coordinator will set up a tickler file and all staff will
> review the residents treatment team plans and will write progress notes.

WHEN WILL IT BE ACCOMPLISHED

> Within the month.

MEASURE TO INDICATE THAT THE PROJECT HAS BEEN COMPLETED OR TO WHAT DEGREE

> Upon notification to the Treatment Team Coordinator through the Director of
> Resident Services of those residents who participate and are not included on
> the Treatment Plan. After it has been documented as an objective then monthly
> charting on intergrated progress notes can begin.

JANUARY 1982

NAME OF PROJECT: IMPLEMENTATION OF DOSP - To outline a method for Resident Involvement

GOAL#2

WHAT WILL BE DONE

> To determine a criteria for referrals and resident involvement in Work
> Activities

HOW IT WILL BE DONE

> Using various criteria lists and other objective tools for evaluating potential
> referral to workshop

WHO IS GOING TO DO THIS

> Director of Resident Services and Work Activities Coordinator

WHEN WILL IT BE ACCOMPLISHED

> March 1983

MEASURE TO INDICATE THAT THE PROJECT HAS BEEN COMPLETED OR TO WHAT DEGREE

> Teams will begin utilizing written criteria; referrals will be more
> appropriate

JANUARY 1983

Goals and Objectives (Chart Format)

_____ Dept./Unit

Quarterly Review – 1st 2nd 3rd 4th

GOALS & OBJECTIVES (include projected achievement date)	RESPONSIBLE INDIVIDUAL	EVALUATION DATE	HOW TO BE EVALUATED BY WHOM	EVALUATION FINDINGS BY THE EVALUATOR	IMPACT/COMMENTS ADDITIONAL PLAN

SERVICE/DEPARTMENT EVALUATION FORM

Rehabilitation Services UNIT/DEPT

QUARTER: 1st 2nd 3rd 4th
(CIRCLE ONE)

ADMINISTRATIVE & CLINICAL GOALS 1980-1981

GOALS & OBJECTIVES (include projected achievement date)	RESPONSIBLE INDIVIDUAL	EVALUATION DATE	HOW TO BE EVALUATED BY WHOM	EVALUATION FINDINGS BY THE EVALUATOR	IMPACT/COMMENTS ADDITIONAL PLAN
Objective I: Develop an Occupational Therapy Department 1. Create and hire 8 OTR's	Administration Gail Fidler	9/30/81 2/30/81	Staff on payroll G.S. Fidler	8 registered occup. therapists on payroll 2/30/81	
2. Implement Services in: Gero Psy. Program C Main Building Medical Services	J.—O.T. Dir. J.—O.T. Dir. J.—O.T. Dir. J.—O.T. Dir.	9/30/80 9/30/80 2/30/81 5/30/81	G. Fidler Program review and documentation via schedules, attendance, etc.	Achieved 9/30/80 Achieved 10/15/80 Achieved 2/30/81	3 programs in place—positive feedback—evidence of more need in Gero.Psy. Unit
3. Implement evaluation process	J.—O.T. Dir.	3/80/81	G.S. Fidler, Protocol developed, documentation in charts	Program C completed 2/30/81, Main Bldg. partial 2/30/81—Gero-Psy. partial 3/21/81	Documentation improved— Treatment referrals improving
4. Staff participate in Treatment Planning	J.—O.T. Dir.	3/15/81	G. Fidler Staff Schedules-Team-Check	All staff on team. 3/15/81	Insufficient staff to cover all teams—Need for O.T. in Medical Services
5. Establish protocol for referrals and programs	J.—O.T. Dir.	4/30/81	G. Fidler Written protocols & standard referrals	Completed and in manuals 5/20/81	
6. Integrate O.T. and Activity Programs	J.—O.T. Dir. J.—O.T. Dir.	4/30/81	G. Fidler Coordinating Committee developed, program & staff schedules	Committee is operating schedules coordinated 3/15/81	

cc: Quality Assurance

PSYCHIATRIC HOSPITAL

ADMINISTRATIVE & CLINICAL GOALS 1980-1981

SERVICE/DEPARTMENT EVALUATION FORM

UNIT/DEPT _____

QUARTER: 1st   2nd   3rd   4th
(CIRCLE ONE)

GOALS & OBJECTIVES (include projected achievement date)	RESPONSIBLE INDIVIDUAL	EVALUATION DATE	HOW TO BE EVALUATED BY WHOM	EVALUATION FINDINGS BY THE EVALUATOR	IMPACT/COMMENTS ADDITIONAL PLAN
7. Establish In-Service education program.	J.--O.T. Dir.	4/30/81	G. Fidler Program schedule and implementation	One program completed others being finalized 5/20/81. compl. 5/20/81	
8. Establish and hire 3 additional OTR's, Gero-Psy. & Medical Services	Administration G. Fidler	6/30/81	Staff on payroll	Not achieved, position not available	Gero-Psy. and M.S. in critical need--re-establish positions as priority goal, 1982
Objective II: Improve breadth & quality of Vocational Rehabilitation Goals:					
1. Document assessments on all referred patients.	J.--Voc. Rehab. Dir. J.--O.T. Dir.	4/15/81	Utilization Review G.S. Fidler	Completed--up-to-date 5/30/81	
2. Improve staffing by adding: Instructor Counselor On-Job Instructor Occupational Therapist Rehabilitation Counsel	Administration T.--Voc. Rehab. Dir.	4/30/81 9/30/81 4/30/81 4/30/81	G.S. Fidler Staff on payroll	3/20/81-Request in process 9/7/81--on payroll 3/20/81--in process 1/2/81--2 on grant project	
3. Seek Grant Funding	T.--Voc. Rehab. Dir.	6/30/81	G.S. Fidler Project submitted	3/20/81--Project submitted	6/1/81 Grant approved
4. Increase number of patients in program to 100	T.--Voc. Rehab. Dir.	3/30/81	G.S. Fidler Documentation monthly reports.	Achieved 6/30/81	1981-82 increase 25%

cc: Quality Assurance

121

State of New Jersey
Department of Human Services
Division of Mental Health and Hospitals

REHABILITATION SERVICES

Monthly Report Protocol

The Rehabilitation Services MONTHLY REPORT FORM is to be used by the Rehabilitation Department/Services to report services provided to patients.

The report form contains a statistical section and a narrative section.

Statistical Data Section

Services/Department: Each department within Rehabilitation Services will complete a Monthly Report Form. In instances where services are purchased through an outside agency, it is the responsibility of the Supervisor of Rehabilitation Services or designee, to compile the data and complete the Monthly Report Form.

Patient Living Units: Data in this category should reflect the name or other designation of the unit from which referrals are being made.

No. Referrals: Record the number of referrals received from each of the units.

No. Initial Assessments: Record the number of initial assessments completed.

Program Components: This section records the program/activity categories and/or treatment procedures provided and the total number of patients in each program/ activity or treatment. Some examples of program components are:

ADL programs
Compensated workshop
Pre-voc
On-the-Job Training
Active sports
Mobility training
Voc. Ed.
Self medication
Remedial reading

Direct Patient Contact Hours: This figure reports the time period in hours and fractions of hours during which the patient received a service. It should not reflect the number of staff or the number of patients participating. For example, 4 hours of individual patient counseling is counted as 4 direct patient contact hours; 6 hours of group counseling for twenty patients is to be counted as 6 direct patient contact hours; and 3 hours of counseling provided by a team of two staff members for 10 patients is to be counted as 6 direct patient contact hours.

Final Summary/Recommendation: Records the number of final summaries and recommendations that have been completed and forwarded to the unit treatment team.

Due Process: This category is specific to Schindenwolf V. Klein relative to curtailment of a work assignment.

Dropped out: Records the number of patients who have unofficially left the program.

Discharge from the Hospital: Records the number of patients who have been discharged from the hospital.

Average Hospital Census: This statistic records the average number of patients in the hospital on a single day (30 days of census added and then divided by 30 = average hospital census).

Total Number of Individual Patients: This statistic records the total number of patients participating in programs during the month and is the sum of new patients and the number of continuing patients.

Percentage of patient population being served: This figure is the total number of patients participating in program services divided by the average number of patients in the hospital (census) multiplied by 100.

122

Total Direct Patient Contact Hours: This statistic records the total DPCH which
is arrived at by adding the figures in the DPCH column.

Total Number of Staff: Record the total number of full-time and/or full-time
equivalant staff.

Narrative Section:

Plans/Changes: Should briefly describe significant changes in programs or staff
as well as those plans for additions or changes that have been finalized.

Highlights: Significant and noteworthy events.

Staff: This section should list the number and kind of positions in the department/
services.

Facility_____   Month of_____ ' 19____

Service/Department_____

Patient Living Units												Total No PTS	Total *DPCHs
No. Referrals													
No. Initial Assessments													
PROGRAM COMPONENTS:													
Final Summary/Recom.													
Due Process													
Dropped Out													
Discharge from Hospital													

Average Hospital Census:_____   Total No. Staff_____
Total No. individual patients:_____   Total DPCH's*_____
  No. new patients:_____
  No. continuing patients:_____
Percentage of patient population being served:_____

   *Direct Patient Contact Hours

124

<u>Narrative</u>:

    <u>Plans/Changes</u>:

    <u>Highlights</u>:

    <u>Staff</u>: (Position titles and number in each title)

_____
Department Head

I. PROGRAM INCOME

    A. Sub-Contract Income

Specify Contract	Total $ Income	Total $ Pat. Payroll	# of Pat. Involved	Total Hours Involved	Other Expenses	Net Balance
Name of Company _____ Type of Contract _____ This Month Year to Date						
Name of Company _____ Type of Contract _____ This Month Year to Date						
Name of Company _____ Type of Contract _____ This Month Year to Date						
Name of Company _____ Type of Contract _____ This Month Year to Date						

126

B. State Budgeted Training/Employment Allocations

Specify Program/s	Total Allocation	Total $ Salary to Patient	# of Patients Involved	Total Hours Involved	Net Balance
_____ This Month Year to Date					
_____ This Month Year to Date					

II. Overview of Patient Involvement

Unit	On Grounds									In Community		
	Central			Satellite			Work Adjustment					
	# of Pat.	Hours	$	# of Pat.	Hours	$	# of Pat.	Hours	$	# of Pat.	Hours	$

I. PROGRAM INCOME

A. Sub Contract Income – Annual Totals

# of Contracts	Total # Patients Served	Total Pat. Payroll	Other Expenses	Balance	Total Income

B. State Budgeted – Training/Employment Resources

	Total # Patients Served	Total Pat. Payroll	Other Expenses	Balance	Total Allocation
Training					
Employment					

C. Grants (specify each grant separately)

Type and Source of Grant	Purpose of Grant	RESOURCES			Total Allocation
		Total # of Staff	Total Salary for Staff	Total Amount for Equipment and Supplies	

D. Other Income (specify source/amount/and utilization)

Grand Total of Income _____

II. EXPENDITURES

A. Program Staffing

Position Title	#	Program Assignment	Total Annual Salary	Pt/Ft Tem/Perm

A. Program - Staff Salaries   Sub-Total   _____

B. Equipment/Supplies
       (Specify)

          Purchase   _____

          Installation/Repair/Service   _____

          Lease   _____

                 Sub-Total Equipment/Supplies   _____

C. Transport Costs
       (Specify)

                                        _____
                                        _____
                                        _____

                 Sub-Total Transportation   _____

D. Miscellaneous Expenditures
       (Specify)

                                        _____
                                        _____
                                        _____

                 Sub-Total Miscellaneous   _____

                 Grand Total Expenditures   _____

III. BALANCE

     Grand Total Income Less   _____

     Grand Total Expenditures   _____

                                Balance   _____
                                                         ===================

130